BUSINESS ETHICS

FOR B.B.A. (3RD SEMESTER) OF BHAGAT PHOOL SINGH WOMEN'S UNIVERSITY, KHANPUR

ANNU SEHRAWAT

ISBN 979-888546760-5

THE CONSTITUTION OF INDIA

PREAMBLE

WE, THE PEOPLE OF INDIA, having solemnly resolved to constitute India into a SOVEREIGN SOCIALIST SECULAR DEMOCRATIC REPUBLIC and to secure to all its citizens:

JUSTICE, social, economic and political;

LIBERTY of thought, expression, belief, faith and worship;

EQUALITY of status and of opportunity; and to promote among them all

FRATERNITY assuring the dignity of the individual and the unity and integrity of the Nation;

WE DO HEREBY GIVE TO OURSELVES THIS CONSTITUTION.

Contents

Foreword

BPS University, Khanpur has revised the course contents of BBA course. This book has been especially written for the new syllabus of Paper Code : BBL - 101 "Busniess Ethics".

I have received Valuable suggestions from Dr. Prashant Kumar, Department of Management, Govt P.G. Collage, GOHANA for the first two units of the syllabus. Therefore, I owe special thanks to Dr. Prashant Kumar for his constructive guidance and support in writing this book.

I am sure that this book would be very useful both students and teachers. Suggestions and critical comments for improvement of the book are welcome.

Author

Website : annusehrawat8520.blogspot.com

E- Mail : annusehrawat8520@gmail.com

Preface

First credit goes to my teachers who have always inspired me ("**Dr Prashant Kumar**", "**Mr. Kapil**", "**Mrs. Babita More**").

Second credit to **my parents**. Who always supports me.

Author

Prologue

SYLLABUS

BPS UNIVERSITY

BBA (3rd Semester)

BUSINESS ETHICS

Paper Code : BBL - 101

UNIT - 1

Business Ethics : Concept, Principle of personal ethics, principle of professional ethics, role and importance of business ethics, Evaluation of business ethics, Benefits from managing ethics in workplace, Characteristics of ethical organizations, values and ethics in business, code of cundect and ethics for managers, Walton's six modules of business cundect, Why should business act ethically.

UNIT- 2

Concept and theories of business ethics : Normative theories, Utilitarianism, Kantian ethics, Stockholder theory, stakeholder theory, Social contract theory, Creating an ethical organization, Social Audit; Ethics and teaching in religion; Indian ethical traditions; Gandhian principles of trusteeship

UNIT - 3

Ethical Decision- Making: Ethical modal for decision making, process, Ethical Dilemma : concept, structure

UNIT 4

Globalization and Business Ethics : CRT, Stakeholders, Employee, owner,

Environmental Ethics Ethics of consumer protection, Marketing Ethic

CHAPTER ONE

Nature of Business Ethics

The nature and concept of Ethics, we can say that Business Ethics is nothing but the application of Ethics in business. Business Ethics proves that businesses can be, and have been, ethical and still make profits. Business Ethics was thought of as being a contradiction of terms. Thankfully, not any more. Today, more and more interest is being given to the application of ethical practices in business dealings and the ethical implications of business.

Human beings have been endowed with the freedom of choice and the means of free will. He can distinguish between good and evil, right and wrong, just and proper. He can distinguish between the end he wishes to pursue and the means to gain that end.

Now, what is true for human beings is also true for business, because business are carried on by human beings only, and business organisations are nothing but formal structures for human beings to carry on their businesses. Moreover, businesses are thought of as being living, growing entities. Thus, businesses also have choices-a choice to maximise their profits and a choice to do good for the society in which they live and operate.

However, at most times, profit maximisation and discharging of social responsibilities at the maximum limit, cannot be carried on simultaneously. One is bound to affect the other. For example, Concern for Task (Productivity) and Concern for Human Beings (workers) are bound to pull each other in opposite directions. It is difficult, if not impossible, to maximise both together.

A conflict arises in trying to achieve both simultaneously. Hence, many managerial choices represent Managerial Dilemmas, between the profit consideration (commercial concern) and the social consideration (welfare concern) of the organisation. Many managerial decisions have ethical implications and these decisions give rise to Managerial Dilemmas.

For example, ruining occupations of age-old inhabitants in a particular locality and their ethical way of life, by using advanced technology, is an ethical dilemma. Technological advancements have to come, have to be used; however, what to do with the people whose life and earnings are affected by the utilisation of advanced technology, is a question which is difficult to answer.

Recently an award-winning regional language file of India, depicted the plight of an aged boatman whose occupation was to transport people and goods across the local river, as there was no bridge over the river. However, his occupation gets threatened when a bridge is built over the river.

This does not mean that technology advancement must not be utilised or that modern methods should not be welcomed. Certainly, they should. Science and technology should, by all means, be used to uplift and make better the lives of human beings all over the world, and specially in such backward regions as this boatman lived.

However, consideration should also be given to see whether alternative means of arrangements can be made so that people are not unduly disturbed or that their trauma and upheaval is kept at a minimum. In case of the boatman, an ethical and effective solution lies in providing him with alternative employment on the bridge itself-as a security man, toll tax collector, etc.

Similarly, when Mergers take place between companies, or Acquisition of one company by a bigger company, where Job positions are duplicated, instead of employees losing their jobs for no fault of their, ethical solutions lies in Job Reassignment or Retraining for alternative Job Assignments.

A business or company is considered to be ethical only if it tries to reach a trade-off between perusing its economic objectives and its social obligations, i.e., between its obligations to the society where it exists and operates; its obligations to its people due to whom it can even think of pursuing economic goals; to its environment, from whom it takes so much without it demanding anything back in return; and the like.

What are the obligations of a business, is open to interpretations. The list of obligations that a company must perform is long and complex and hence, are costly to the company; yet they must be discharged, if a company wants to survive and grow in the long run and is not satisfied in making profits only in the short ran. While discharging its obligations to the society, the company not only fulfils its own duties, but also paves the way for a stronger and more ethical foundation.

Definitions:

According to Andrew Crane,

"Business ethics is the study of business situations, activities, and decisions where issues of right and wrong are addressed."

According to Raymond C. Baumhart,

"The ethics of business is the ethics of responsibility. The business man must promise that he will not harm knowingly."

Scope of Business Ethics

- Ethics In Compliance
- Ethics In Human Resource
- Ethics In Finance
- Ethics In Production
- Ethics In Marketing

- **Ethics In Compliance**

Business ethics play an efficient role in the compilation of business activities with legal rules and regulation. It ensures that business adheres to all established laws and any of its operations don't go unlawful. It reduces any chance of facing any unfavourable action by authorities like payment of fines and penalty. Business following ethics in their operations frames strategies and policies in accordance with established rules and regulations. All activities are monitored and ensured that they go in accordance with framed policies.

- **Ethics In Human Resource**

Human resources are the key element of every business and have an important role in its success. Ethics helps in improving the employer-employee relations and overall productivity of the business. Ethics related to human resource are introduced and implemented by Human resource management in business. HRM covers all ethical issues related to employer-employee affecting their relationship.

The various issues covered are Discrimination issues, sexual harassment, employee's privacy issues, salaries and wages issues, safety and health issues. Ethics aims at overcoming all these issues so that employees are happy and motivated towards their roles. This booms the overall performance and reduce the risk.

- **Ethics In Finance**

Finance is a crucial part of every business and is needed for its successful operations. Finance should be properly managed by every business otherwise it may have adverse effects. Ethics aims at controlling and handling all finance issue faced by companies and employees. The various ethical issues included are accounting related like window dressing and improper window dressing, insider trading, fake reimbursements, overbilling, bribery, kickbacks etc.

- **Ethics In Production**

Ethics in business helps in monitoring and controlling the overall production activities. It ensures that production processes do not adversely affect the business. Ethics frames production policies by considering organisation goals, objectives and various environmental factors.

Attempts are made to minimise the degree of risk and danger. The various ethical issues covered are defective and dangerous products, environmental ethics and pollution issues, Issues arising out of new technologies and product testing issues. Implementation of ethics controls these issues and fosters overall productivity.

- **Ethics In Marketing**

Marketing is an important part of every business organisation. It is the means through which it improves the sales and profitability of the business. Marketing practices should be ethical and should avoid the adoption of any unfair means.

Implementation of ethics ensures that all marketing programmes are moral-ethical. The various ethical issues covered are pricing issues like price discrimination and price skimming, misleading advertisements, black marketing, anti-competitive practices, wrong advertisement content etc.

Nature of Business Ethics

- Contains Rules And Principles
- Voluntary
- Avoids Cheating And Frauds
- Education And Training Required
- Dynamic Concept
- Social Welfare
- New Concept

- **Contains Rules And Principles**

Nature of Business Ethics defines the code of conduct for every business. It tells various rules and principles that every business should implement in its operations. Business is easily able to decide what is wrong and what is right for its growth and goodwill by adopting these ethics. Business ethics are applicable and required to be followed by every individual working in the business organisation.

- **Voluntary**

Business ethics are moral principles and social values that are not enforceable by law. These ethics are required to be adopted by businessmen by their own will. Business ethics brings self-discipline within the business environment. Businessmen should understand the relative importance of these ethics and adopt them hassle-free.

- **Avoids Cheating And Frauds**

Ethics in business keeps an eye on every activity of the business. It ensures that no malpractices take place within the business organisation. Rules and principles provided by these ethics focus on that business does not indulge in any unfair practises like black marketing, adulteration, misleading advertisement, inaccurate weight measures, misleading advertisement etc. Every employee working with a business need to respect these ethics, failure of which leads to a penalty.

- **Education And Training Required**

Proper education and training should be provided to businessmen and people working with business before ethics implementation. A proper explanation should to be provided to all so that they are fully aware of the benefit of these ethics. Once they are informed about these ethics advantages, they will be self-motivated to adopt these. There should be an active role of commerce chamber and trade associations for in this regard.

- **Dynamic Concept**

Business ethics is a dynamic concept and changes from time to time for the welfare of the business. Ethics differs from business to business as per the nature and type of business. It also differs from region to region and country to country. Business ethics are designed in accordance with culture, traditions and religions of a particular area. Same business ethic may be good for one region and a taboo for another region.

- **Social Welfare**

Ethics in business provides a framework for the welfare of society and peoples associated with it. These ethics ensures that business should not exist for its growth only but should also work for upliftment of its stakeholders. Business should provide fair wages and better working condition to its employees, fair payment of taxes to the government, transparency of information to shareholders and taking part in various amenities for society.

- **New Concept**

Business ethics is a new concept. It is not mandated by any law to be followed by every business. In developed countries, business ethics are followed strictly. Whereas in poor and developing countries these are not followed properly.

Characteristics of Business Ethics

- Defines Code Of Conduct
- Protects Social Group
- Control Business Malpractices
- Related To Moral And Social Values
- Requires Willingness To Accept
- Creates Good Image
- Relative Term
- Requires Education And Guidance

- **Defines Code Of Conduct**

Business ethics defines the code of conduct for every business. It clearly defines the activities that business should adopt in its code of conduct. Ethics states what is right or what is wrong for a business and what a business should do or what it should not do for its growth and welfare of society. It provides basic framework for doing a business. Ethics defines social, cultural, economic, legal and other limits of business and they should operate within these limits.

- **Protects Social Group**

Business ethics provide protection to different social groups associated with business. Implementation of ethics in business ensures that it does not operate only for its growth but should also consider the welfare of social group. Needs and rights of customers, employees, government, shareholders, creditors, small businessmen etc. are given equal importance along with their own goals by business. Business adopting and following ethics therefore gives protection to all social groups.

- **Control Business Malpractices**

Business ethics monitors and keeps a check on any malpractices in business. It ensures business performs all activities ethically without getting involved in any unfair trade practices. Business ethics avoids adoption of unfair trade activities like adulteration, black marketing, frauds and cheating in product, improper weights and measures etc. Controlling of all these malpractices by ethics helps in maintaining the legality of business.

- **Related To Moral And Social Values**

Ethics in business are based on moral principles and social values. These ethics states that business should operate morally without exploiting others. Business should not only focus on its profitability or growth but also work for the betterment of its stakeholders. Ethics in business includes self-control, providing service to society, consumer welfare and protection, treating social groups fairly, not exploiting others, etc.

- **Requires Willingness To Accept**

Implementation of business ethics requires the willingness to accept by businessmen. This is the basic requirement for successful adoption of ethics by any business. Ethics are voluntary in nature and are not enforceable by any law. These ethics must be adopted like self-discipline by businessmen at their own choice.

- **Creates Good Image**

Business ethics has an important role in improving the goodwill of the business. Ethics defines rules and regulation that it need to adopt in its operations. It ensures that business maintain certain standards in their code of conduct. They should use better technology and resources for their production processes. Providing quality products at fair prices helps in serving and satisfying customers in a better way. This enhances the overall goodwill of business organisation in the market.

- **Relative Term**

Business ethics is a relative term and it changes from business to business. Business ethics are not the same for every organisation. It changes from organisation to organisation and from country to country. Business ethic that may be good or moral in one country may be treated as taboo in other countries.

- **Requires Education And Guidance**

For proper adoption of business ethics, it is required to educate and guide businessmen about them. Before introducing ethics businessmen should be properly taught about the benefits of these ethics. They should be motivated to implement these ethics by explaining their advantages. Trade Associations and Chambers of Commerce should take an active role in educating businessmen.

Features of Business Ethics

- Maintains Legality Of Business
- Reduce Risk And Cost
- Providing Quality Products
- Healthy Competition
- Profit Making
- Good Employer-Employee Relations
- Long Term Growth

- **Maintains Legality Of Business**

Business ethics ensure that business does not involve in any illegal activities. Ethics in business clearly defines the rules and principles that business needs to adopt in its code of conduct. These ethics avoid the adoption of unfair trade activities like adulteration, black marketing, frauds and cheating in the product, improper weights and measures etc. This all helps in maintaining the legality of the business.

- **Reduce Risk And Cost**

Ethics in business helps in improving the productivity and overall efficiency of the organisation. These ethics bring self-discipline within the organisation and aims at reducing the risk and expenses. All the people working in an organisation are strictly required to follow these ethics and are imposed to a penalty in case of any failure. Employees are required to strictly required to focus on their defined roles for achieving higher efficiency.

- **Providing Quality Products**

Quality products are a must for keeping the customers happy and satisfied. Ethics in business defines certain standards for the production of better products for customers. Businesses are required to use better technology and resources for manufacturing their products. They should not comprise with product quality and should meet the standards level set by these ethics.

- **Healthy Competition**

Unhealthy competition in the market makes the condition worse for the existence of the small business. Every business should adopt fair market practices for healthy competition in the market. They should cooperate with their business partners and other business organisation existing in the market. Ethics in business focuses on that any business organisation does not aim at creating its monopoly in the market by exploiting other ones existing in the market.

- **Profit Making**

Business ethics are not against the profit earning objective of business. The aims that business should not earn profit by unfair means. Businessmen should remain honest and not cheat its customers, investors and employees. Involvement in any fraudulent activities for raising profit should be avoided.

- **Good Employer-Employee Relations**

Implementation of ethics in business makes the employer and employee relations better. These ethics ensure that business should not operate for its own growth only but also work for the welfare of its employees. All employees should be provided better and timely wages and salaries, proper working conditions and various other amenities. It helps in developing better relations and understanding among employer and employees.

- **Long Term Growth**

Ethics in business focuses on the survival of business organisations for long term. Business cannot exist for long term if any of its operations leads to exploitation of its stakeholders. These ethics ensure that business works for the welfare of all its stakeholders and tries to achieve their support. With the support of all its stakeholders business can easily touch the height of great success and can continue its operations for the long-term.

Advantages and Disadvantages of Business Ethics

Advantages of Business Ethics

1. **Enhance Business Reputation:**

Business ethics helps in enhancing the reputation of the organization in the market. Practicing of ethics ensures the legality of business and provide better service to customers. It controls all unfair trade practices and operates all activities ethically. The business operates at a lower profit level and delivers quality goods. This develops a positive image of the company and attracts a large number of new customers.

1. **Positive Work Environment:**

It helps in maintaining a positive work environment for business. Ethics clearly defines the code of conduct for business and directs the limits within which it should operate. Employees are trained to work efficiently in a team and develop better relationships with their co-workers. Superiors trust their subordinates and grant them proper autonomy for performing their roles effectively.

3. **Improves Customer Happiness:**

Ethics leads to improve customer satisfaction with the business. Companies follow ethical principles operate at a reasonable profit and fulfill all needs of their customers at a lower cost. Customers when treated fairly get committed to the business for the long term. They get proper help support and all their complaints are redressed timely. Business via these good ethical principles are able to build a loyal customer base.

4. **Retain Good Employees:**

Adopting of ethical principles enable business in retaining good employees for a longer period. Employees want to work with such an organization that treats them fairly and recognizes their talent. They need to be compensated for their work and wants appreciation based on their work quality. Companies dealing with their workers fairly and openly are able to easily retain them.

5. **Builds Investor Loyalty**:

All investor wants to be associated with the ethical business for earning better return. They look for reputation, ethics, and social responsibility of business before choosing the one to invest their funds. Business working on ethical values are able to attract large number of investors. Investors know that ethical values enable organization in enhancing their productivity, efficiency, and profits.

6. **Avoid legal Problems:**

Controlling legal issues is another important advantage provided by business ethics. Implementation of ethical principles ensures that organizations comply with all labor laws and environmental regulations. Employees are provided safe working environment and good quality materials for carrying out the operations. Companies maintaining proper ethical standards avoids themselves from any fine and penalties charges by government agencies.

Disadvantages of Business Ethics

1. **Reduce Profits:**

Business ethics reduces the profit earning ability of the organization by putting limits to its operations. Companies working on ethical values can't focus on profit maximization by exploiting others. They need to give equal attention to the interest of its stakeholders like customers, employees, society, creditors, and government. Business running on an ethical path needs to forego extra profits which adversely affect their growth and revenue.

2. **Time Consuming:**

Implementation of ethics within the business practices is a time-consuming process. It is a long process that requires large efforts on the part of the organization. Businessmen need to properly learn about these ethics for their successful implementation.

3. **Not Ideal for Small Business:**

Ethical standards are not suitable for small scale business as it lower their profit. Small business cannot afford to lose some profit for the sake of running their operations ethically. It can hamper their growth and survival in today's stiff competition. Following these principles brings extra cost to the business which is not feasible for small companies.

4. **Instability:**

Business ethics are not stable and are changed from time to time. Business owners revise them as per the company needs and desires without considering whether they are ethical or not. It becomes inconvenient to change these standards within the business practices many times. Companies needs to educate and guide its employees each time it brings changes to its standards.

CHAPTER TWO

Functions of Business Ethics

Functions of Business Ethics

1. **Protect consumer rights:**

Business ethics ensures that customers are treated fairly and provided with their full rights. Organizations that implement ethics operates economically and provide better quality goods at lower cost. They serve customers at a reasonable profit without exploiting them. Customers are fully satisfied with services that makes them loyal to such businesses for a long term.

1. **Enhance relations with society:**

Relationship with society is must for survival of every business organization. Ethics directs business to consider the interest of society and work for their welfare. It should not focus only on its growth at the cost of exploitation of society. Business should actively participate in corporate social responsibility and should contribute towards infrastructural development programmes for its society.

3. **Safeguard interest of industry**:

Business ethics protects the small scale business from exploitation by large firms in an industry. It provides them full rights to operate efficiently and establish their position in market. Following of ethics in an industry ensures that all firms works fairly without the exploitation of other players in market.

4. **Improve business goodwill:**

Ethics play a key role in enhancing the overall image of business in market. It monitors all operations of business and avoids any unethical activities. Practicing of ethics maintains the legality of business thereby providing better service to customers. All unfair trade activities are controlled and quality goods are delivered. Customers are happy with the services which leads to create a positive image of company.

5. **Assist in decision making:**

Supporting in decision making of organization is an important function played by business ethics. Ethics provides rules and guidelines to be followed by business in its functioning. All decisions are taken in light of moral and social values mentioned in these ethics. It guides in deciding what is right or wrong for business organization. Every ethic need to be practiced properly and any violation will lead to penalty.

Importance of Business Ethics

1. **Control Business Malpractices:**

Business ethics directly influence the operations of the business. It is the one which helps business in deciding what is wrong and what is right. These ethics set certain rules and principles to be followed strictly by business, and their violation leads to a penalty. Implementation of these principles ensures that business does not indulge in any unfair practices like black marketing, providing misleading advertisement, frauds in measures and weight, adulteration, etc. Through business, ethics works on providing better products to its customers at reasonable prices.

1. **Better Relation with Employees:**

Employees are an important part of the business and necessary for the survival of the business. Business ethics ensures that business works for the welfare of its employees working with it. The business should not only work for the achievement of its objectives like profit maximization and higher growth but should also focus on peoples working with it. These ethics ensures that business provides better monetary compensation and good working conditions to its employees, active participation in decision making, addressing complaints, and providing promotions as per their progress. This helps in maintaining a good relationship with employees.

3. **Improves Customer Satisfaction:**

The consumer is termed as king in the market and is the one who decides the success or failure of every business. It is important that the business fulfills the needs of its customers. Business ethics provides principles for business operations under which it is required to provide better quality products at reasonable prices. It ensures that the business provides better customer support and redressal of all complaints. This helps businesses in improving the satisfaction levels of its customers.

4. **Increase Profitability**:

Business ethics improve the productivity and profitability of every business. It sets certain rules to be followed by every person working with the business. Every employee is required to adhere to these rules and should focus on its duties with sincerity. These ethics ensure that there is no wastage of resources, and every resource is efficiently utilized. This eventually leads to an increase in business profit in the long run.

5. **Improves Business Goodwill**:

Business goodwill has an important effect on capturing the market. Better goodwill businesses are able to attract more and more customers. By implementing ethics in its operations business aims at providing better service to the market. Businesses that work ethically operate at the low-profit base and with honesty. This develops a better image in front of the public and is easily accepted by customers with fewer efforts.

6. **Better Decision Making:**

Ethics in business helps them in making better decisions timely. It provides certain rules and guidelines that every business needs to follow in its operations. Every decision is taken in light of the moral principles and social values provide through these ethics. It helps businesses in deciding what is right and what is wrong. Every person working within the business is required to respect these ethics, violation of which would lead to the penalty.

7. **Protection of Society:**

Society is very important for the success of every business. If a business does not consider the interests of its society, then it will harm its survival. Business ethics direct that business should work for the welfare of its society and take part in various infrastructural development programs.

It ensures that business contributes actively to its corporate social responsibility. A business should not perform any activity that creates a problem for the society in which business exists.

Types of Business Ethics

1. Personal Responsibilities
2. Official Responsibilities
3. Corporate Responsibilities
4. Economic Responsibilities
5. Legal Responsibility
6. Personal loyalties
7. Organizational loyalties

8. Technical morality

1. **Personal Responsibilities:**

Personal responsibilities refer to the personal code of ethics of an individual which he follows firmly in his daily activities. Such ethics are: always behaving honestly, respecting elders, performing accepted duties properly and timely, promptly settling all dues, not indulging into criminal activities etc.

2. **Official Responsibilities:**

These are the responsibilities which comes with the position that a person occupies. Every official position has certain rules and regulation that are meant to be strictly followed in all situations. An individual holding such a position should follow all standards and norms set for that particular official position.

3. **Corporate Responsibilities:**

Corporation is an artificial person which is treated as a separate legal entity. They have their own moral responsibilities towards the society that is distinct from personal moral ethics of managers running them. Such responsibilities are both internal and external which assists in deciding matters related to employees, shareholders, customers, creditors, society and government.

4. **Economic Responsibilities:**

These ethics are one which guides actions of an individual which are of economic nature. Economic responsibilities consist of moral values which directs toward the usage of resources. Every business should make efficient use of all resources and try to enhance the profitability without involving in any fraud. They should avoid any kind of wastage and contribute towards the welfare of society.

5. **Legal Responsibility:**

Legal responsibilities provides a framework within which a business should operate. It shall abide by all the rules and regulations imposed by legal authority. All unethical activities should be avoided as they are treated as illegal in eyes of law.

6. **Personal loyalties:**

It means the loyalties that superiors have towards thier subordinates and loyalty that subordinates have towards their superiors. If a superior act honestly and treats its subordinates fairly, then the subordinates will not face any problem. Similarly, the subordinates having strong personal loyalty for their superior will turn blind eyes towards the blunders of their superior.

7. **Organizational loyalties:**

This involves the loyalty of employees towards their organization. Some employees develop a deep sense of loyalty out of love and affection for the organization. Such loyalties are so strong that they even do not hesitate from neglecting their personal interest for the sake of organization. They work efficiently toward the achievement of organizational goals.

8. **Technical morality:**

Technical morality is related to state of technology implied by enterprise for production of its goods or services. Every professional person having technical morality shall not compromise with quality of goods. They should properly adhere to all the ethical standards provided by competent bodies. Organizations focusing on technological advancement are able to attain better efficiency and create more challenging situation for competitors.

Business Ethics Important Principles

Business ethics refers to basic guidelines to study and analyse a sense of right and wrong and goodness and badness of our tasks.

In context of business performance, there are certain principles and guidelines, based on ethical conducts as given here:

1. Principle of Conscience – This principle is based on inner-feeling of persons to analyse the sense of right and wrong. On this basis the businessmen can determine different roles and behaviour at their levels.

2. Principle of Wishless Work – This principle emphasise that there is no need to perform all the task to be self-centered or self-interest. Accordingly, we should perform all the role and behaviour to another person's for their esteemed interest. We should be devoted to our efforts to do the work for others.

3. Principle of Esprit – According to this principle businessmen should give due attention to make best possible services and try to develop the feelings of devotion and truthfulness in services. All the behaviour and activities should be based on values and service motive in business.

4. Principle of Publicity – According to this principle, all the activities and performance as conducting in business houses, should be well informed to every person or organisation who are directly or indirectly attached with business. It aims to remove the doubtfulness and misunderstanding among people.

5. Principle of Purity – It is most needful that every businessman should follow the politeness, truthfulness and tolerance for developing the feelings of mental peace. At the same time, the mental peace and purity also becomes the ways for politeness and tolerances etc.

6. Principle of Humanity – It is needful that every businessman should follow the human values, human decorum and human aspects within their policies, programmes and different working areas. The ethical behaviour may determine the path of humanity.

7. Principle of Universal Values – It is required that every businessmen should conduct and perform the task and different business activities to be based on universal assumptions, customs and overall accepted norms and principles by society.

8. Principle of Commitment – According to this principle, every businessmen should be able to fulfill their commitments and assurances as given to other persons. The implementation of commitments should be based on honesty and responsiveness.

9. Principle of Rationality – On the basis of the ethical code of conduct, every businessmen should analyse and evaluate the good or bad, right or wrong, ethical or unethical aspects within their business transaction and day to day working of the business houses. They must follow the rational attitudes and behaviour.

10. Principle of Communicability – According to this principle, there is a need to make effective means of communication with the internal and external persons as engaged with business houses. The communication should be in cleared, open and justified manners.

11. Principle of non-Cooperation in Evils – It is needful that businessmen should try to make non-cooperation or discourage the evils, misconduct and unethical behaviour not only with different customers but with society also.

12. Principle of Cooperation with Other – Ethical norms motivate the feeling of collaboration and team spirit. It is required that on the basis of capacity and available resource, the businessmen should make full cooperation to different other persons as per their good conduct and value based behaviour.

13. Principle of Satisfaction – Every businessmen are required to create and develop their role and behaviour to establish pleasure and happiness with other persons and the society at large. Fore mostly, in business as per their products and services, the customers should be satisfied at every stage.

14. Principle of Coordinate Ends and Means – The businessmen should try to make a coordinating or balancing form between their ends and means within their work performance and its allied activities. They should develop their ventures within the limitations of resources and capacities.

15. Principle of Due Process – All the persons and different employees, as engaged in business are required to involve in decision making process and different important task. Businessmen should follow a reasonable and justified working process in their organisation.

16. Principle of Liking in Expectations – In order to establish the ethical norms and conducts in business, it is required to follow all these good and acceptable behaviour by businessmen. They must give and perform some excellence examples as per the expectations of others.

17. Principle of Transparency – Ethics denotes the concept of purity and truth. All the business activities and transactions should be well informed with justified manners with their different stakeholders and society.

PRINCIPLES OF PERSONAL ETHICS

Personal values are the conception of what an individual or a group regards as desirable. Personal ethics refer to the application of these values in everything one does. Personal ethics might also be called morality, since they reflect general expectations of any person in any society, acting in any capacity. These are the principles we try to instil in our children, and expect of one another without needing to articulate the expectation or formalize it in any way.2 The principles of personal ethics are:

- Concern and respect for the autonomy of others.
- Honesty and the willingness to comply with the law.
- Fairness and the ability not to take undue advantage of others.
- Benevolence and preventing harm to any creature. ...

Principles of Professional Ethics

Members of NEAFCS will:

- Adhere to the highest standards of professional conduct
- Strive for impartiality and objectivity when dealing with others
- Communicate openly and honestly with colleagues and clientele
- Maintain confidentiality in professional relationships
- Fulfill commitments in a reliable, responsive and efficient manner
- Be fully accountable for actions, use of resources and financial dealings
- Avoid potential or apparent conflicts of interest
- Show respect and understanding toward all people and honor diversity
- Continue to upgrade professional competences to meet changing needs of families and communities

Approved by NEAFCS Executive Board Dec. 2004

Difference between Personal and Professional Ethics

Ethics can generally be described as your sense of right and wrong or good and bad. Ethics can give real guidance o your life. It's an engineer's responsibility to make things better and solve the problems around the world. Some of the importance of ethics in engineering is are :

- Engineering Projects Can Have an Immediate Impact On People's Safety
- It Gives Them Ability To block Against Bad Decisions
- Ethics Have To Be Explained to AI Systems

Ethics can vary wildly from place to place, and person to person. There are many kinds of ethics to categorized and Personal Ethics and Professional Ethics are a major part of it. In this tutorial, we will be studying personal and professional ethics and the difference between them.

1. Personal Ethics :

Personal Ethics refers to a person's personal morals and code of conduct. From the very beginning of a person's understanding, these ethics are being instilled in the individual by their parents, family and friends. Without any personal ethics, the life of the human being is incomplete and shallow. As an example, we can consider an individual's honesty, openness, sense of responsibility etc. The person with good personal ethics will automatically show his moral and virtues while talking to his friends, relatives and elderly people. A person's personal ethics are revealed in an exceedingly professional situation through his behaviour.

2. Professional Ethics :

Professional ethics refers to a person's values and principles that are introduced to an individual in a professional organization.

Each employee in the organization has to follow these rules and they do not have any choice. These ethics are very important to import in the professional world as it helps in bring the sense of disciple into the person's life and maintain the decorum of the organization. As an example, transparency, confidentiality, fairness etc fall under the terms of professional ethics.

Personal v/s Professional Ethics :

The major difference between personal and professional ethics is the strictness with which the individual conform to them. As in personal ethic the values and principles are limited to yourself, it comes under your decision to follow them or not in certain situation. But in the case of professional ethics, the principles and rules must be followed by you otherwise it can badly affect your status and reputation in the organization.

CHAPTER THREE

Evolutions of Business Ethics

- **Business Ethics in the '60s**

The 1960s brought the first major wave of changes in business ethics. Cultural values were shifting, with individualism and fierce dedication to social issues such as environmentalism and world peace coming into vogue.

While young workers in the 1960s were idealistic and wanted to make the world a better place, employers found their work ethic, compared to that of previous generations, was lacking. Drug use was rampant, and the new focus on individualism caused many workers to look upon their employers with disdain.

Companies responded to the changing times by beefing up human resources departments, establishing mission statements, and outlining codes of conduct. In response to the changing desires of their employees, however, businesses also began embracing social responsibility at a level not previously seen. In fact, the 1960s saw businesses trumpet environmental friendliness for the first time and companies also looked for new ways to give back to their communities.

- **Major Events in the ’70s and ‘80s**

During the 1970s and 1980s, two events shaped changes in business ethics: defense contractor scandals that became highly publicized during the Vietnam War and a heightened sense of tension between employers and employees. In response, the government implemented stricter policies governing defense contractors, and companies revamped contracts with employees to focus less on rigid compliance and more on values. Popular management philosophy shifted from pure authoritarianism towards more collaboration and working on equal footing.

- **The ’90s and Environmentalism**

The 1990s saw a rebirth of environmentalism, new heights in social responsibility reaching, and graver legal ramifications for ethical missteps. Tobacco companies and junk food manufacturers, for example, faced heightened scrutiny, along with several important lawsuits over the public health ramifications of their products. Oil companies and chemical companies had to contend with increasing public pressure to answer for environmental damage. Class action lawsuits rapidly gained in popularity and, in response, businesses were forced to spend more on legal departments.

- **The Online Realm in 2000+**

From the year 2000 forward, business ethics have expanded to the online realm. The big ethical dilemmas of the 21st century have mostly centered on cybercrimes and privacy issues.

Crimes such as identity theft, almost unheard of 20 years before, are a threat to anyone doing business online. As a result, businesses face social and legal pressure to take every measure possible to protect sensitive customer information. The rise in popularity of data mining and target marketing has forced businesses to walk a fine line between respecting consumer privacy and using online activities to glean valuable marketing data.

CHAPTER FOUR

Benefits from managing ethics in workplace

Benefits from managing ethics in workplace

1. Attention to business ethics has substantially improved society.

A matter of decades ago, children in our country worked 16-hour days. Workers' limbs were torn off and disabled workers were condemned to poverty and often to starvation. Trusts controlled some markets to the extent that prices were fixed and small businesses choked out. Price fixing crippled normal market forces. Employees were terminated based on personalities. Influence was applied through intimidation and harassment. Then society reacted and demanded that businesses place high value on fairness and equal rights. Anti-trust laws were instituted. Government agencies were established. Unions were organized. Laws and regulations were established.

2. Ethics programs help maintain a moral course in turbulent times.

Attention to business ethics is critical during times of fundamental change — times much like those faced now by businesses, both nonprofit or for-profit. During times of change, there is often no clear moral compass to guide leaders through complex conflicts about what is right or wrong. Continuing attention to ethics in the workplace sensitizes leaders and staff to how they want to act — consistently.

3. Ethics programs cultivate strong teamwork and productivity.

Ethics programs align employee behaviors with those top priority ethical values preferred by leaders of the organization. Usually, an organization finds surprising disparity between its preferred values and the values actually reflected by behaviors in the workplace. Ongoing attention and dialogue regarding values in the workplace builds openness, integrity and community — critical ingredients of strong teams in the workplace. Employees feel strong alignment between their values and those of the organization. They react with strong motivation and performance.

4. Ethics programs support employee growth and meaning.

Attention to ethics in the workplace helps employees face reality, both good and bad — in the organization and themselves. Employees feel full confidence they can admit and deal with whatever comes their way. Bennett, in his article "Unethical Behavior, Stress Appear Linked" (Wall Street Journal, April 11, 1991, p. B1), explained that a consulting company tested a range of executives and managers. Their most striking finding: the more emotionally healthy executives, as measured on a battery of tests, the more likely they were to score high on ethics tests.

5. Ethics programs are an insurance policy — they help ensure that policies are legal.

There is an increasing number of lawsuits in regard to personnel matters and to effects of an organization's services or products on stakeholders. As mentioned earlier in this document, ethical principles are often state-of-the-art legal matters. These principles are often applied to current, major ethical issues to become legislation. Attention to ethics ensures highly ethical policies and procedures in the workplace. It's far better to incur the cost of mechanisms to ensure ethical practices now than to incur costs of litigation later. A major intent of well-designed personnel policies is to ensure ethical treatment of employees, e.g., in matters of hiring, evaluating, disciplining, firing, etc. Drake and Drake (California Management Review, V16, pp. 107-123) note that "an employer can be subject to suit for breach of contract for failure to comply with any promise it made, so the gap between stated corporate culture and actual practice has significant legal, as well as ethical implications."

6. Ethics programs help avoid criminal acts "of omission" and can lower fines.

Ethics programs tend to detect ethical issues and violations early on so they can be reported or addressed. In some cases, when an organization is aware of an actual or potential violation and does not report it to the appropriate authorities, this can be considered a criminal act, e.g., in business dealings with certain government agencies, such as the Defense Department. The recent Federal Sentencing Guidelines specify major penalties for various types of major ethics violations. However, the guidelines potentially lowers fines if an organization has clearly made an effort to operate ethically.

7. Ethics programs help manage values associated with quality management, strategic planning and diversity management — this benefit needs far more attention.

Ethics programs identify preferred values and ensuring organizational behaviors are aligned with those values. This effort includes recording the values, developing policies and procedures to align behaviors with preferred values, and then training all personnel about the policies and procedures. This overall effort is very useful for several other programs in the workplace that require behaviors to be aligned with values, including quality management, strategic planning and diversity management. Total Quality Management includes high priority on certain operating values, e.g., trust among stakeholders, performance, reliability, measurement, and feedback. Eastman and Polaroid use ethics tools in their quality programs to ensure integrity in their relationships with stakeholders. Ethics management techniques are highly useful for managing strategic values, e.g., expand marketshare, reduce costs, etc. McDonnell Douglas integrates their ethics programs into their strategic planning process. Ethics management programs are also useful in managing diversity. Diversity is much more than the color of people's skin — it's acknowledging different values and perspectives. Diversity programs require recognizing and applying diverse values and perspectives — these activities are the basis of a sound ethics management program.

8. Ethics programs promote a strong public image.

Attention to ethics is also strong public relations — admittedly, managing ethics should not be done primarily for reasons of public relations. But, frankly, the fact that an organization regularly gives attention to its ethics can portray a strong positive to the public. People see those organizations as valuing people more than profit, as striving to operate with the utmost of integrity and honor. Aligning behavior with values is critical to effective marketing and public relations programs. Consider how Johnson and Johnson handled the Tylenol crisis versus how Exxon handled the oil spill in Alaska. Bob Dunn, President and CEO of San Francisco-based Business for Social Responsibility, puts it best: "Ethical values, consistently applied, are the cornerstones in building a commercially successful and socially responsible business."

9. Overall benefits of ethics programs:

Donaldson and Davis, in "Business Ethics? Yes, But What Can it Do for the Bottom Line?" (Management Decision, V28, N6, 1990) explain that managing ethical values in the workplace legitimizes managerial actions, strengthens the coherence and balance of the organization's culture, improves trust in relationships between individuals and groups, supports greater consistency in standards and qualities of products, and cultivates greater sensitivity to the impact of the enterprise's values and messages.

10. Last – and most — formal attention to ethics in the workplace is the right thing to do.

Characteristics of an Ethical Organization

We hear a lot these days about how organizations are striving to balance the need to reach lofty revenue and profit goals with the desire to create a culture built on a foundation of ethics and integrity. This raises an important question: What exactly is an "ethical" culture?

According to Dr. Albert C. Pierce, Director of the Institute for National Security Ethics and Leadership, the most ethical organizations are the ones that are able to develop these four abilities in their employees: moral awareness, moral courage, moral reasoning and moral effectiveness.

The National Association of State Boards of Accountancy views an ethical culture as one that is able to integrate two distinct systems: ethical culture, which focuses on teaching employees specific organizational values and the importance of "doing the right thing;" and ethical climate, which emphasizes the development of ethics-related attitudes, perceptions and decision-making processes throughout the organization.

Regardless of how one defines the concept of an ethical culture, the organizations that have the most success in creating and sustaining an ethics-based environment tend to adhere to best practices in the following 10 areas, as identified by Kirk O. Hanson, Executive Director of the Markkula Center for Applied Ethics at Santa Clara University:

1. **Strong Values Statement**

A values statement is a short, concise encapsulation of what the organization stands for, the values that its employees are expected to embody and what its products/ services are intended to contribute to the world. In the most ethical organizations, these statements become deeply ingrained principles that serve as guideposts for employee and organizational decisions and actions.

1. **Well-Crafted Code of Conduct**

A code of conduct is a written set of principles that works in tandem with the values statement to serve as an ethical roadmap for the organization. The best codes of conduct are comprehensive, well-organized documents that are written in plain, understandable language instead of legalese. Developing a code of conduct is a multi-step process that typically requires extensive input from all areas of the organization.

3. **Leading by Example: Executive Modeling**

It is often said that ethics starts at the top. Even a well-crafted values statement and code of conduct won't be worth the paper they are written on unless top executives "live and breathe" the principles they espouse on a daily basis. An excellent way for CEOs, CFOs and other key executives to set an ethical tone is by sharing examples of situations they've faced that posed an ethical dilemma, and how they chose the proper path when making their decisions.

4. **Comprehensive Ongoing Ethics Training**

Too many organizations only provide ethics training to brand-new employees. Ongoing training is also essential for firmly embedding ethics into the culture. The training should consist of much more than an online course that provides a quick review of fundamental ethics principles. It should encompass a thorough review of the code of conduct and the organization's specific ethics policies and procedures. It should also include case studies and real-world scenarios that enlighten employees as to how to make ethical and values-driven decisions relative to their specific job functions. It is also advisable to conduct separate training for ethics and compliance.

5. **Integration of Values into Work Processes**

Any work process that organizations develop should include references to values and how they impact the decisions that pertain to the system. A good way to achieve this is by incorporating an ethics/values component into the employee performance evaluation process with a focus on how workers have applied ethics to their decision-making processes.

6. **Establishment of a Confidential Reporting Mechanism**

Even organizations that make ethics a top priority are likely to experience ethical breaches and instances of inappropriate behavior at some point. Establishing an anonymous third-party reporting hotline provides employees with a confidential mechanism for informing designated personnel within the organization whenever they witness or are the victims of wrongdoing. A hotline can be an extremely effective tool for stopping misbehavior in the early stages, before it can escalate into a major issue.

7. **Transparent Investigative Process for Ethics Violations**

Employees will be reluctant to use a hotline if they believe that their reports will simply disappear at the bottom of a desk drawer. The most ethical organizations have a mechanism in place to conduct a prompt, thorough, transparent investigation of all hotline reports so that the issue can be resolved in an equitable, timely manner. The administration of fair, just disciplinary action is also critical. The organization's values message will surely be lost if top managers receive lighter punishments than front-line personnel for the same inappropriate behavior. Providing protection for whistleblowers against retaliation is also essential component of the investigative process.

8. **Effective Ethics Governance**

Best practices stipulate the appointment of a dedicated corporate ethics and compliance officer (CECO), a senior executive who oversees the ethics function and plays a key role in establishing the organization's ethical compass. This individual should be given wide latitude to develop and implement ethics policies and procedures. Creating an ethics committee that reports to the board of directors is another effective corporate governance step.

9. **Periodic Revision of Ethical Standards**

It is important to review the ethical standards at periodic intervals to ensure they continue to meet the organization's needs and to gain a fresh perspective on the overall effectiveness of all ethics initiatives. Hanson recommends a comprehensive revision of the standards every three years that takes into account any new ethical challenges the organization faces. It should also include an evaluation of any ethical breaches that may have occurred since the previous review.

10. **Unwavering Focus on Constant Improvement**

It's easy for an organization to become satisfied with the status quo in terms of ethics, especially when no significant breaches have occurred over an extended period of time. However, when an organization lets its guard down and reduces the level of focus it places on ethics, it has the unwanted effect of fostering a culture that invites unethical behavior. The most ethical organizations are constantly seeking ways to keep ethics and compliance at the forefront of every action they take.

In conclusion, it should be noted that creating an ethical culture isn't easy, and it doesn't happen overnight. However, those entities that stay the course and endeavor to adapt these 10 characteristics stand an excellent chance of developing and implementing a culture of ethics that permeates every level of the organization.

CHAPTER FIVE

Code of Conduct for Managers

Value and Ethics in Business

Values and ethics in simple words mean principle or code of conduct that govern transactions; in this case business transaction. These ethics are meant to analyse problems that come up in day to day course of business operations. Apart from this it also applies to individuals who work in organisations, their conduct and to the organisations as a whole.

We live in an era of cut throat competition and competition breeds enmity. This enmity reflects in business operations, code of conduct. Business houses with deeper pockets crush small operators and markets are monopolised. In such a scenario certain standards are required to govern how organizations go about their business operations, these standards are called ethics.

Business ethics is a wider term that includes many other sub ethics that are relevant to the respective field. For example there is marketing ethics for marketing, ethics in HR for Human resource department and the like. Business ethics in itself is a part of applied ethics; the latter takes care of ethical questions in the technical, social, legal and business ethics.

Code of Conduct for Managers

A code of conduct is important for managers in every industry, as a workforce can't move forward without integrity from its leaders. The best managers place a high value on fairness and ethics, as well as their own performance. Not only do managers who create their own code of conduct benefit their workers, but they also often benefit the entire company's public image.

Honesty

Managers in every industry must understand their company's policies and guidelines, as well as its mission, and how they are expected to go about accomplishing their goals. They also need to know and follow the laws of the government, particularly as they pertain to business. Mostly, effective managers must be honest about aspects such as production and profit at all times. While being dishonest isn't always a federal offense, it can result in numerous issues for a company.

Accountability

Good managers expect their workers to take responsibility for their actions and overall performance, and demand the same of themselves. That means answering to ownership or executive boards when things don't go right, accepting the blame, and coming up with solutions to avoid future issues.

Integrity

Managers who perform their jobs with a high level of integrity are widely the best type of supervisors to work for. That's because managers who possess integrity are often consistent in their decision-making and resolution of issues. These managers also make their goals clear and assist employees when it comes to reaching those goals.

Respect

Appropriate behavior is a key factor in a code of conduct for a manager, who must demonstrate acceptable behavior in the workplace. That doesn't mean managers need to act like robots and display little signs of personality. Quite the opposite, actually, as many managers are expected to be energetic and lead in areas of teamwork and motivation. But they also need to treat staff members, customers and their own supervisors with the same respect they would expect for themselves.

Flexibility

While most companies don't expect their managers to display sympathy to employees who aren't meeting expectations, most businesses prefer leaders who are patient and work with those in need of assistance. Good managers show their workers how jobs are best performed, then monitor workers and offer suggestions and tips. After all, the goal of managers in every industry is to make sure workers stay productive and the company stays profitable.

why should businesses act ethically

An organization has to be ethical in its behaviour because it has to exist in the competitive world. We can find a number of reasons for being ethical in behaviour, few of them are cited below: Most people want to be ethical in their business dealings. Values give management credibility with its employees. Only perceived moral righteousness and social concern brings employee respect. Values help better decision making.

There are a number of reasons why businesses should act ethically:

- to protect its own interest;
- to protect the interests of the business community as a whole so that the public will have trust in it;
- to keep its commitment to society to act ethically;
- to meet stakeholder expectations;
- to prevent ...

CHAPTER SIX

Walton's six models of business conduct

Walton's six models of business conduct

All businesses must meet certain standards of law and minimum cultural standards. All are further influenced by the general cultural aspects of their time. But in spite of these tendencies uniform conduct, there are important differences among business. Each has its own personality, as each human being does. These organizational differences are reflected in company codes of conduct and they do produce different results. As a guide to understanding different types of business conduct, Walton classifies six models of conduct. Those are Discussed bellow:-

(a) The austere model: It gives almost exclusive emphasis to ownership interest and profit objective. In this model, a business firm exclusively emphasizes owners ' interest and the profit motive.

(b) The household model: The concept of extended family this model emphasizes employee job, benefits, and paternalism. The firm adopting this model employs a paternalistic approach with its employees.

(c) The vendor model: In this model, consumer interest, tastes, and rights dominate the organization. In this model, the interests and rights of customers are given top priority.

(d) The investment model: This model focuses on the organization as an entity and thus on long-term profits and survival. Social investment is given recognition along with economic investments.

(e) The civic model: its slogan is corporate citizenship. It goes beyond imposed obligations, accepts. This model makes a positive commitment to social needs its slogan is corporate citizenship and social responsibility is accepted.

(f) The artistic model: This model encourages the organizations to become creative instrument serving the cause of an advanced civilization with a better quality of life. Creative ideas are generated and used for this purpose.

The six models may be thought of as points on a continuum from low to high social responsibility.

CHAPTER SEVEN

Business Ethics Theories

Types of Business Ethics Theories

Business Ethics theories form the foundations for acceptable behaviors and decisions in the work environment. For some professionals, their business values may run parallel to their religious codes of conduct. The majority of **professional ethics** are based on the idea of doing what is best for the group and focusing on the moral aptitude of the action, rather than the result. The three main business ethics theories are **deontological theory, utilitarianism, and norm theory.** One of the largest influences of modern business ethical principles is Kantian theory, which is a type of norm theory.

Deontological theory states that ethical behavior should follow an established set of rules or principles in all types of situations. Even though the actual outcome of following established moral principles may differ, the result does not determine whether the action is ethical. For example, according to deontological theory, it would always be unethical to lie even if lying would prevent an unfavorable consequence, such as death.

Utilitarianism is the idea that business conduct should take into account the consequence that would benefit the largest amount of people. As far as business ethics theories are concerned, it is one that is probably open to a great amount of interpretive differences. For example, in international commerce, the consequences of the decision to impose tariffs might be more beneficial to the group of people on one particular side of the transaction. In addition, it could be argued that the decision's consequences might benefit the largest amount of people in the short-term, but harm a greater amount in the long run.

Norm theory states that certain standards of moral conduct should be followed by the entire group. The acceptable forms of conduct are typically defined for a variety of probable situations. A prime example of norm theory in the business world is the idea of employee handbooks or corporate codes of conduct. These usually provide a framework for how employees should respond and behave in given circumstances, with deviation from the code resulting in disciplinary action.

Business ethics theories related to norm theory include Kantian ethical principles. These principles were developed by a Russian philosopher and theorist who proposed that ethical guidelines should speak to humanity as a collaborative group. Business ethics theories based on Kant's philosophy should treat humans as ends rather than as means. In other words, when developing a code of conduct, an individual should not use others to serve his own purpose or advantage.

Stakeholder Theory

Stakeholder Theory is a view of capitalism that stresses the interconnected relationships between a business and its customers, suppliers, employees, investors, communities and others who have a stake in the organization. The theory argues that a firm should create value for all stakeholders, not just shareholders.

In 1984, R. Edward Freeman originally detailed the Stakeholder Theory of organizational management and business ethics that addresses morals and values in managing an organization. His award-winning book Strategic Management: A Stakeholder Approach identifies and models the groups which are stakeholders of a corporation, and both describes and recommends methods by which management can give due regard to the interests of those groups.

The theory has become a key consideration in the study of business ethics and has served as a platform for further study and development in the research and published work of many scholars, including those featured on this website.

Since the 1980s, there has been a substantial rise in the theory's prominence, with scholars around the world continuing to question the sustainability of focusing on shareholders' wealth as the most fundamental objective of business.

We aim to be the hub of leading stakeholder research and thinking by providing resources to new scholars, students, and business leaders.

Social contract theory is an ancient philosophical idea that states that an individual's ethical and political obligations relate to an agreement he has with every other individual within a society. The agreement can be written, as in the form of laws, or it can be a tacit agreement, an unspoken or unwritten agreement of social norms and customs. In business, social contract theory includes the obligations that businesses of all sizes owe to the communities in which they operate and to the world as a whole. This involves corporate philanthropy, corporate social responsibility and corporate governance.

creating an ethical organizational

1. Walk the talk – be a role model

The most effective way for leaders to inspire ethical conduct in employees is to demonstrate it every day in their own behaviour. This means asking the right questions to arrive at ethically informed decisions, getting all the facts about allegations of misconduct, and being willing to say no to business practices (and business partners) that conflict with the stated values of the organisation, regardless of how lucrative they might appear.

Simply put, there is a human dimension to corporate ethics and compliance, which concerns the personal integrity, judgement, and competence of an organisation's people – most importantly the CEO and senior leadership team.

2. Incorporate ethics into hiring, promotion and reward

Reshaping a culture also requires changing how employees are hired, promoted, and rewarded. Looking at a candidate's ethical track record is an essential component of due diligence, and should not be an afterthought in seeking out the best and the brightest. Ethical performance should also be a core consideration in promoting employees to positions of greater responsibility and prestige. Furthermore, if an organisation fails to visibly reward people for good behaviour (and sanction them for bad behaviour), the integrity culture begins to erode, and the unrelenting drive for profit and growth can cloud judgment and lead to ethical lapses.

3. Don't allow double standards

CEOs sometimes have ethical blind spots, especially around the conduct of their most ambitious, high-achieving subordinates. Highly intelligent, charismatic employees are often allowed to operate largely unchecked; their departments and business units sometimes become semi-autonomous kingdoms lacking sufficient central oversight. I call these potentially dangerous characters the 'superstar managers'. Part of leading by example means holding these high performers accountable for their actions and not allowing ethical double standards to persist and undermine the organisation.

4. Communicate your expectations

This means that there must be clear, consistent, and frequent communication of the organisation's integrity standards and expectations to all its stakeholders, including third-party business partners. Communication can take many forms – for example, events such as town halls provide a visible platform for setting the 'tone at the top' as well as enabling open, two-way dialogue on ethical issues. It's also important to introduce mandatory ethics and compliance training for all employees. In a global organisation, it's critical to tailor ethics and compliance training by region rather than following a 'one-size-fits-all' approach; training materials need to reflect local cultural contexts and risks, and incorporate relatable dilemma scenarios and lessons learned from past lapses.

5. Promote a speak up culture

Corporate leaders should do everything in their power to encourage a 'speak up' culture and investigate all allegations that come to them. Whistle-blowers help bring vision to the wilfully blind; the messages they send should never be ignored or suppressed. As a leader, it's essential to remember that whistle-blowers are not the enemy. There are too many corporate boards and senior executives who think their companies are doing well because there have been few allegations raised. It is more likely that the lack of allegations is evidence of a serious problem. Allegations are important signals about the health and culture of a company, including the openness of communication. People should feel safe enough to make them, and leaders need to be wise enough to act on them.

It may seem obvious that ethical transformation begins with leadership. However, in practice, senior executives and Board members too often view ethics and compliance as a niche functional concern, or a series of talking points, or a hindrance to strategy and growth; and this viewpoint impedes efforts at reform. Incentivising ethical conduct is an essential component of infusing integrity throughout the fabric of your organisation; in the long run, it will make for a more profitable, resilient, and sustainable business.

CHAPTER EIGHT

Social Audit

A social audit can be defined as a review of a company's production procedure, policies, and code of conduct to find how they impact society. It is conducted out of social responsibility by an organization to establish its positive image in public, and if anything is found negative, then suitable actions are taken to correct them.

Social Audits

The meaning of social audit is to inspect a company's working and production procedure to improve its social performance. The output of the social audit provides information on how well a company is keeping a balance between social responsibility and making profits.

Social audit is mandatory to be conducted as a company might overlook the social responsibility to make profits. The term "Social audit" is part of business culture since 1950.

Another reason for conducting it is to establish a positive image of the company in society to attract more customers. Companies conduct social audit internally, and if everything is found fine and per the society, then the report is made public.

This not only put a positive impression on the customers of the company but will also attract investors.

Objectives & Management

- To assess the impact of the company's operations on the local community and environment.
- To determine and minimize or eliminate the economic and social gaps.
- To assess the conditions in which workers are made to work.
- To determine whether workers are being paid fair wages or not.
- To determine whether the shareholders of the company are given fair information about the financial status of the company or not and whether they are paid their dividend in the company's income regularly or not.
- To put a stop on irregular activities.
- To formulate and activate initiatives for the development of local communities.
- To Take measures for the extension and development of the company's business.
- To keep the fair price of the goods produced for the consumers.
- To ensure that whether the assets and resources of the company are being used properly or are being wasted.

Importance

Conducting a social audit is important, as an organization not only impact the employees working in it or the consumers who consume products produced by them, but it also impacts the society and people of the local community.

It is conducted so that no powerful organization can exploit the resources available to it and don't use any antisocial means to make a profit. In some countries, a social audit is made mandatory by the government.

However, to make the reports public or not is completely in the hands of the organization. Because of the continuous deteriorating condition of environment and society, the social audit has become essential to curb the antisocial and anti-environment actions of organizations.

In addition to this, a positive report creates a positive image of the company.

conduct the Audits?

Followings are the well-defined steps involved in the social audit.

#1 Define the scope:

Social auditing consists of the auditing of various departments and activities at the same time. Therefore, it is important for the auditor to establish the boundaries that mean he should decide what should be audited and what should not be audited during the auditing process.

The objective of conducting a social audit is to analyze the process implemented for the execution of the process, quality of basic services and infrastructure created, and to assess the health and security measure taken.

#2 Choose the people participating in the process:

In the next step, you will decide who should be included in the process whether they are the management of the organization or stakeholders an also define up to what percent a person would be involved in the process, how often they would be contacted, and what information would be shared with whom?

They can also work as the consultation in the social audit process, make sure that people involved in the process are unbiased and have no personal objectives. The whole purpose of conducting the social audit process should be concerned with the society and environment.

#3 Define the key issues which are required to be cross-checked in the process and a data collection procedure for those issues:

In the next step, key issues which are required to be analyzed and tackled through the social audit process should be defined. Define what information should be collected for the particular issue and what methods should be opted to collect information.

Different records should be analyzed at different point of time to prepare a report.

#4 Generate a report for findings and verify it:

In the next step, you should generate a report about the findings of social auditing. Social auditing reports might be or might not be published. Therefore, It is important to review the report and physically verify the process of important tasks.

Make sure to verify the processes by visiting the workplace; otherwise, a small mistake in the social auditing report might leave the accuracy of the whole report in jeopardy.

#5 Present the report:

The main purpose of conducting a social audit is to present the report about the work process of an organization. The report is presented to designated management or shareholders, and sometimes reports are presented publicly.

However, a company holds the right whether to share report publicly or not. Finally, the required steps are taken to address the issues.

CHAPTER NINE

INDIAN Ethical Traditions

Traditions of ethics

Ethical frameworks involve an overlap of 1) philosophical traditions, 2) religious traditions, and 3) moral principles. Most people will draw from all of these but emphasize one framework or another in their approach to ethics.

1. **Philosophical traditions**

When we are confronted with an ethical dilemma, we often use a combination of ethical tools to understand the situation and judge what is best to do. We think about our duty, about the impact on other people, about whether an action is virtuous or fair. Understanding the range of ethical tools helps us approach ethical challenges in a more thoughtful way. These philosophical traditions in ethics have emerged in various epochs of human history. Virtue ethics is from classical civilizations; Consequence and Duty ethics emerged in the Enlightenment period; Justice ethics emerged in the mid-20th century; and Bioethics became a major concern in the late 20th century.

1. **RELIGIOUS TRADITIONS — BUDDHISM, CHRISTIANITY, HINDUISM, JUDAISM, ISLAM**

Buddhist — Eightfold path: (Right views, Right aspirations, Right speech, Right conduct, Right livelihood, Right effort, Right mindfulness, and Right meditational attainment).

Christian — Includes the Golden Rule (Love your neighbor; Do unto others as you would have them do unto you; turn the other cheek;) and the concept of avoiding sin.

Hindu — Ahimsa, do no harm to any living thing

Islamic — Surrender to the will of God.

Jewish — Ten Commandments (also Christian and Islamic)

3. **Moral Principles**

When making these difficult moral choices, sometimes its helpful to discuss basic moral principles in neutral language that transcends philosophical or religious traditions. According to Gerald Corey, Issues and Ethics in the Helping Professions, (NY: John Wiley & Sons, 1999), terms for basic principles found in ethical traditions are:

Autonomy / people make their own choices without manipulation

Nonmaleficence / do no harm

Benificence / help people

Justice / fairness, treat all people alike

Fidelity / honor commitment to those you serve

Veracity / truthfulness

Trusteeship (Gandhism)

Trusteeship is a socio-economic philosophy that was propounded by Mahatma Gandhi. It provides a means by which the wealthy people would be the trustees of trusts that looked after the welfare of the people in general. This concept was condemned by socialists as being in favor of the landlords, feudal princes and the capitalists, opposed to socialist theories. Gandhi believed that the wealthy people could be persuaded to part with their wealth to help the poor. Putting it in Gandhiji's words "Supposing I have come by a fair amount of wealth – either by way of legacy, or by means of trade and industry – I must know that all that wealth does not belong to me; what belongs to me is the right to an honourable livelihood by millions of others. The rest of my wealth belongs to the community and must be used for the welfare of the community." Gandhi along with his followers, after their release from prison formulated a "simple" and a "practical" formula where Trusteeship was explained. A draft practical trusteeship formula was prepared by Gandhi's co-workers, Narhari Parikh and Kishorelal Mashruwala and it was fine-tuned by M.L. Dantwala.

CHAPTER TEN

ETHICAL DECISION MAKING

Ethical decisions inspire trust and with it fairness, responsibility and care for others. The ethical decision making process recognizes these conditions and requires reviewing all available options, eliminating unethical views and choosing the best ethical alternative.

Good decisions are both effective and ethical. In professional relationships, good decisions build respect, trust, and are generally consistent with good citizenship. Effective decisions are effective when they achieve what they were made for. A choice that produces unintended results is ineffective and therefore not good.

The key to making good decisions is to think about the different choices that lie ahead in order to achieve the objectives. For that reason, it is also very important to understand the difference between short-term vs. medium to long term objectives.

Making ethical decisions requires a certain sensitivity to ethical issues and a method of examining all the considerations associated with a decision. Having a method or structure for making ethical decisions is therefore essential. After this process has been performed a few times, the method is trusted and it is easier to walk through the steps.

Below is a description of ethical decision-making methods.

Framework for ethical decision making

If ethics is not based on religion, feelings, law, social practices or science, what is it based on? Countless philosophers and ethicists have attempted to answer this critical question. At least five different ethical norms or standards have been proposed. The most important are explained below.

The Utilitarian Approach

This approach dictates that the action that is the most ethical is the action that produces the most good and causes the least harm. In other words, the decision that strikes the greatest balance between good and evil.

In a business environment, it is therefore the decision that yields the most benefits and causes the least damage to customers, employees, shareholders, the environment, etc.

The Right Approach

The right approach suggests that the most ethical decision is the one that best protects and respects the moral rights of all concerned. This approach argues that people have a dignity based on human nature or their ability to freely choose what they want to do with their lives.

Based on that dignity, they have the right to be treated equally by others and not just as a means to an(other) end.

The Fairness or Justice Approach

All equals should be treated equally. The Greek philosopher Aristotle and others contributed to that idea. Today, this idea is used to indicate that ethical decisions treat everyone equally. If not equal, this must be based on a standard that is explainable.

People are paid more for their hard work when they contribute more to the organization. That is fair. But many wonder whether the salaries of CEOs, some 100 times higher than others, are fair. Is this standard defensible?

The Common Good Approach

The Greek philosophers also contributed to the idea that living in a community is a good thing. People's actions and actions must contribute to this. This approach suggests that relationships within society are the basis of ethical reasoning and acting. Respect and compassion for all others, especially the vulnerable, are prerequisites for maintaining an ethical way of life.

The Virtue Approach

An ancient approach to ethics is the belief that acting ethically must be in accordance with certain virtues that ensure the development of humanity in general. Virtues are tendencies and habits that enable man to act with the highest potential of human character.

Ethical decision-making process and roadmap

Below is a summary of the roadmap for the ethical decision-making process.

1. Gather the facts

Don't jump to conclusions until the facts are on the table. Ask yourself questions about the issue at hand, such as the 5 whys method. Facts are not always easy to find, especially in situations where ethics plays an important part. Some facts are not available or clearly demonstrable. Also indicate which assumptions are made.

2. Define the ethical issue

Before solutions or new plans can be considered, the ethical issue is clearly defined. If there are multiple ethical focal points, only the most important should be addressed first.

3. Identify the stakeholders

Identify all stakeholders. Who are those primary stakeholders? And who are the secondary stakeholders? Why are they interested in this issue?

4. Identify the effects and consequences

Think about the possible positive and negative consequences associated with the decision. What is the magnitude of these consequences? And what is the probability that these consequences will actually occur? Distinguish between short-term and long-term consequences.

5. Consider integrity and character

Consider what the community thinks would be a good decision in this context. How would you like it if the national newspaper wrote about your decision? What is public opinion? How does your character and personality influence the decision to be made?

6. Get creative with potential actions

Are there other choices or alternatives that have not yet been considered? Try to come up with additional solutions or choices if a small number is considered.

7. Decide on the right ethical action

Consider the options based on each option's consequences, duties, and character aspects. Which arguments are most suitable to justify the choice?

Ethical Decision Making Models

Sometimes, people consider understanding the obligations of public relations professionals as a science. The ability to apply ethical reasoning into a tapestry of various situations, however, is truly an art. In an attempt to address this, many scholars have proposed ethical decision-making processes, based on ethical frameworks previously addressed. The following are three popular models that are designed specifically for professionals to understand how to apply their ethical commitment in action. The following is a brief introduction to these decision-making models:

- **Bowen's Model for Strategic Decision Making:** This model for ethical decision-making is specifically designed to help with issues management. In other words, it helps professionals make correct decisions in a management process in order to avoid ethical problems and crises. In this model, Bowen suggests first ensuring that the professional is autonomous in the decision making process. In other words, it is important in this model that the public relations professional is free of outside influences that may change what choices they would make. Then the model guides the professional into making a decision based on considerations for the key duties to the client and publics. In making the decision, professionals are encouraged to consider whether others in similar situations could be obligated to perform the same way, whether they would still make the same decision if they were on the receiving end of the choice, and whether similar situations like this have been faced before. After making the decision, there is also guidance on how to communicate the choice. Questions that a professional should consider include "am I doing the right thing?" and "am I proceeding with a morally good will?"

TARES Ethical Persuasion: Often, public relations professionals are communicating messages designed to influence values, opinions, beliefs and behaviors. When using persuasive communication, there are certain ethical obligations that the communicator holds. The TARES model is a guide for this kind of communication. TARES, suggests using the following acronym as a guide: "Truthfulness (of the message) Authenticity (of the persuader), Respect (for the persuadee), Equity (of the persuasive appeal) and Social Responsibility (for the common good)." In other words, the public relations professional needs to make sure their communication aligns with each of these five areas prior to using it.

- **Potter's Box for Decision Making:** This is perhaps one of the most simple but often employed models for making ethical decisions. This model was developed by social ethics professor, Ralph Potter and is often used in a variety of professions. This process guides individuals through a four step process involving 1) examining the issue at play in the situation; 2) identifying values that should be employed, 3) recognizing guiding principles and 4) ascertaining loyalties that should be employed. This model is one that rests on professionals understanding principles, values and loyalties in order to be able to navigate the ethical choice correctly.

CORPORATE VALUES AND ETHICAL DECISION MAKING

In a person's work environment, the values, the vision and stated mission of the company where he or she works, have greater influence than his or her own values and moral standards. In organizations, decisions—ethical or otherwise—are made jointly through committees, consultations, discussions or at meetings of groups responsible for particular operations or by getting advice and inputs from experts in the field. The evolved culture and structure of an organization operate through the individual relationships of its members and have an impact on their decisions. Every organization has a culture evolved over the years, or imposed from the top when a new management takes over, and every employee tries ...

CHAPTER ELEVEN

Ethical Dilemma

Ethics are the moral standards and principles by which entities (individuals and organizations) govern their behaviors and decision-making. When these standards and principles conflict with each other in a decision-making situation, an ethical dilemma may occur.

an Ethical Dilemma?

An ethical dilemma takes place in a decision-making context where any of the available options requires the agent to violate or compromise on their ethical standards.

We observe that ethical dilemmas can be characterized by the following three elements:

- The agent must be faced with a choice or the need to make a decision.
- The agent must have more than one course of action available.
- The agent recognizes that all available courses of action require them to compromise on some personally held ethical standard or value.

Ethical standards are the moral frameworks that individuals and organizations use to guide their decision-making and differentiate between right and wrong. Companies and professional organizations may adopt their own ethical standards and require that employees/ members adopt those standards as part of their personal business ethics.

Common ethical practices in the workplace include:

- Telling the truth
- Taking responsibility for one's actions
- Following company policies
- Fulfilling professional obligations
- Following through on commitments
- Following the law
- Acting in the best interests of shareholders
- Acting in the best interests of customers
- Acting in one's own best interests
- Treating others equally
- Conducting sustainable business practices
- Maximizing profits
- Avoiding layoffs

Ethical dilemmas happen because ethics are inherently contradictory. Employees may face situations where compromising on telling the truth or following the law seems to serve other valued goals, such as maximizing profits or avoiding layoffs.

Types of Ethical Dilemma

There are several different types of ethical dilemmas that agents may encounter in the course of performing their roles and responsibilities:

- Epistemic dilemmas take place in a decision-making context where moral standards conflict and the agent cannot readily determine which ethical principle should take precedence over the other.
- A self-imposed dilemma is one created by the agent's own errors in judgment, such as making competing promises to multiple organizations that cannot be fulfilled simultaneously. In contrast, a world-imposed dilemma is caused by circumstances outside the agent's control.
- An obligation dilemma is one where an agent has multiple options and more than one of them is obligatory, while a prohibition dilemma occurs when all available options are prohibited.

Example of an Ethical Dilemma

Ethical dilemmas occur regularly in the business environment where employees make decisions that impact the success and profitability of organizations.

Employees may experience an ethical dilemma when deciding whether to report an incident of workplace harassment or declare a conflict of interest. In the first case, the employee might understand that the harassment is wrong, but feel guilty about getting their colleague in trouble. In the latter case, the employee might recognize their fiduciary duty to the organization, but feel a sense of loyalty to their family and friends that makes it difficult to do the right thing.

Resolve an Ethical Dilemma

An ethical dilemma does not always offer a clear solution that conforms with ethical norms. Here's how entities can cope with the most challenging ethical dilemmas:

- Talk it Out – The best way to determine whether a dilemma exists is to discuss it with other people. A collective analysis of the situation can shed light on whether a dilemma really exists and the moral implications of each available option. This might involve reporting the incident to your company's hotline so that you may discuss the situation with the compliance team and get proper guidance.
- Understand Duties & Obligations – A great way to approach any ethical dilemmas is from the standpoint of understanding the agent's duties in the situation. In a business context, a fiduciary duty to the organizations legally obligates the agent to act in the best interests of shareholders. Contractual obligations can also play a role in determining how to resolve an ethical dilemma.

Maximize the Good & Minimize the Bad – When a problem has no perfect solution, the best approach is to analyze the outcomes of each potential action and choose the action with the greatest positive impact and least negative impact.

Stakeholders & Ethical Dilemmas

The prevalence of major corporate scandals over the years has helped increase public awareness of two major ethics concepts – stakeholders and ethical dilemmas. While these concepts are not unique to the study of business, they tend to be more commonly applied to ethical corporate decision making. For example, the corporate social responsibility movement is a direct application of these ideas in business. But what exactly do they mean?

Stakeholders

Stakeholders are broadly defined as anyone who is impacted by a decision-maker's decision. Some examples of corporate stakeholders would be shareholders, employees, customers, suppliers, financiers, families of employees and the community in which the corporation is located. Stakeholders could also be less directly related to the operations of a corporation. For example, taxpayers who later need to fund a government rescue of a distressed company, the government and even those suffering the effects of corporate pollution are all stakeholders, in that they have a stake in decisions.

Ethical Dilemmas

An ethical dilemma occurs when you have a moral obligation to abide by two different courses of action, but circumstances of the situation only allow for you to choose one of the two courses. An example would be reporting unethical wrongdoing by a boss who is engaged in some form of corporate fraud. Many employees in this situation would be conflicted in their fear of losing their jobs, making it difficult for them to meet obligations to provide for their families. However, by not reporting the wrongdoing, they put other stakeholders in jeopardy.

Stakeholders and Ethical Dilemmas Applied

Identification of potential stakeholders is essential for ethical behavior. Failure to identify stakeholders has led many to make unethical decisions without realizing they had a moral dilemma in the first place. For years companies adhered to the purpose of making profit, legally. At first blush, this sounds reasonable and moral; however, it has also led to many corporate scandals where companies toed legal boundaries and though they never crossed statutory limitations, their poor decision-making hurt many millions of stakeholders. For instance, for many decades paper companies routinely and legally polluted rivers and lakes, making the water undrinkable for humans and uninhabitable for fish and animals.

Dealing With Ethical Dilemmas

Unfortunately, there is no perfect method for dealing with ethical dilemmas. Regardless of your choice, you will need to face and accept the consequences of your actions. However, there are two ways to look at your situation to help you come to a decision. The first way is to evaluate the potential actions you can take and then pick the course that is least morally problematic. The second involves analyzing the potential outcomes of your actions and selecting the course of action with the most benefits or least harm.

SOURCES OF ETHICAL PROBLEMS

According to Keith Davis and William C Frederick5 ethical challenges in business take several forms and raise different kinds of ethical dilemmas. Ethical challenges and their attendant dilemmas may arise due to (i) failure of personal character; (ii) conflict of personal values and organizational goals; (iii) organizational goals versus social values; and (iv) hazardous, but popular products. Added to these, there may arise other ethical challenges when corporations cross boundaries and become multinational companies. Newer technologies, diverse religious, cultural and social beliefs, different economic systems, political systems and ideologies may bring in their own dilemmas and problems.

CHAPTER TWELVE

code of personal ethics for employees

A code of ethics is a set of principles for employees to adhere to when conducting business to comply with company standards. A business code of ethics, usually based on the core values of the business, outlines the company mission statement, how professionals should approach dilemmas and the standards to which they hold their employees. An individual's code of ethics can include their beliefs, values and background.

While codes of ethics are unique to every individual or organization, they commonly reflect an overall idea of what the general population considers "right" and "wrong" behavior, and many are based upon societal expectations, such as those that teach us not to steal from others.

Having a code of ethics holds a different level of importance for people, but there are clear advantages to creating a personal code of ethics. Since personal beliefs are usually the foundation for an individual's code of ethics, they may refer to it when they are morally unsure about a situation. Their code of ethics can guide to steer them toward an action or opinion that aligns with what they believe on a fundamental level. A code of ethics reinforces individual values and can provide clarity and strength to follow the path they believe is best.

create a personal code of ethics

Follow these steps to create a personal code of ethics:

1. Determine your purpose for writing a personal code of ethics

Establish your personal reasons for developing this code. You may want to do it to guide your behavior in day-to-day situations or to serve as an inspiration to help you embody the kind of person you want to be. Understanding your individual reasons will help you shape your code of ethics, creating a set of principles tailored to your life, beliefs and needs.

2. Make a list of your traits

Write down the traits that you strongly believe represent you as a person. These can include personal traits, such as honesty, kindness, integrity or any other characteristic you associate with your behavior. Ask yourself if people close to you would agree with your assessment. By determining your traits, you can create a more definite and honest code of ethics.

3. Consider your relationships

Imagine individual relationships you have with others and determine what you would like to change about each one. If you work closely with others, determining the quality of your relationships will allow you to create a statement for how you want to maintain or improve them.

4. Create a set of statements to follow

Develop a list of statements that can serve as a guide for what sorts of actions you will take to meet your own expectations. Incorporate your current traits as well as the traits you want to embody going forward in your life.

5. Develop guidelines

Create clear guidelines, or rules, that you intend to follow when interacting with other people on a day-to-day basis. You might also include definitive personal statements that can serve to remind you of the importance you place on applying your personal code of ethics to your life.

CHAPTER THIRTEEN

create and maintain an ethical workplace culture environment

Here are six simple ways in how to create and maintain an ethical workplace culture environment:

1. Integrate core values into the day-to-day

Without core values, it's nearly impossible to create an ethical workplace culture. Core values educate employees, clients, and prospects about where the organization is going and communicate what's most important to the organization. Internally, core values are created to build a sense of trust with your employees and shape the organizational culture. They also create a sense of clarity and purpose for the workforce to be clear on what they need to work towards every day.

Defining and publishing core values alone aren't enough. You have to live them every day—starting with the behavior at the top. Get your executives involved from the beginning when establishing your core values, so they have more ownership over them.

Companies must continue to communicate and educate employees about these core values and ensure they are reflected in and discussed in everything from interviews with potential new hires, onboarding new hires, company-wide meetings, and individual one-on-one sessions. That way, everyone is reminded of the company culture and seeing behavior that is aligned with these values.

Below are examples of core values that these companies have established to create and maintain an ethical workplace with employees and customers:

- Integrity: We are honest, open, ethical, and fair. People trust us to adhere to our word—Adidas
- Green: We strive to minimize our negative impact on the environment—Ben and Jerry's Ice Cream
- Genuine: We're sincere, trustworthy and reliable—Adobe

Once these values are set and shared across the organization, a process must be established to hold employees accountable for any actions which cross ethical violations. With this process, it can help influence and motivate positive behavior, keeping your employee's away from potential ethical violations.

2. It begins at the top

Now that your core values are all set, your job is done. Not quite. To make sure employees are motivated to live your company's core values, executives and managers must live it and model the same behavior they expect in their teams. Leaders must be vigilant about their actions and how their employees interpret them.

If a manager behaves unethically, so will the employees—it's a domino effect. Cutting corners to reach a goal, lying about metrics and numbers to the CEO, and engaging in verbally abusive behavior are just a few examples of how leaders can violate ethical behavior. If employees are noticing these behaviors, they will either think it's okay to do and mirror that behavior or find it offensive and ultimately lose trust in the manager and company overall.

As an HR professional, you can equip leaders with the tools and resources they need to influence and sustain ethical behavior. Ethical leadership must find opportunities to discuss ethical dilemmas in daily work, such as how to avoid cutting corners to meet a tough deadline and seeking help to finish a project on time without forcing team members to do so. Executive influence is vital, and one of the best methods to ensure employees are following company guidelines and being ethical in their day-to-day work.

3. Reinforce the message

While it might take some time for executive influence to kick in, as an HR leader, your job is to continue educating employees. You've communicated company core ethics and values in the workplace via email, on the company website, in company-wide meetings, and during the onboarding process of new hires. Unfortunately, even with all that, employees forget what the core values are, and you see more ethics violations in the workplace, and many are even asking the HR department, "Where can I find our core values?"

Continue the conversation about how ethical behavior aligns with the company's core values. Reinforce the message in a variety of ways, such as training and workshops that teach how to solve ethical dilemmas, open door lunch and learn sessions to discuss potential ethics violations, and internal company newsletters that highlight ethical behaviors, to name a few. Make your team meetings interactive by role-playing examples of ethical vs. unethical behaviors in the workplace and positive reinforcement vs. negative consequences people face. Encourage top executives to speak about company values as well. Another great way to reinforce the message is by posting your core values and ethical guidelines all over the office. That way, if an employee asks, "Where can I find our core values?" you can easily point to them.

4. Create a safe, open space for communication

A safe, open workplace culture motivates ethical behavior. If ethics violations are happening, employees should feel safe to bring it up. According to SHRM, "more than 1 in 5 workers who reported misconduct said they suffered retaliation as a result, up from 12 percent in 2007. A third of those who declined to report the misconduct said they feared they would be punished for doing so."

Bringing up a potentially unethical issue is a sensitive subject and can make employees feel uncomfortable when talking about it. Employees might think that it's not worth bringing up or will lead to a harsh and annoyed reaction from a manager. Companies need to live up to maintaining an open space for employees to communicate freely when they see workplace issues.

Workshops and training sessions come in handy to set the expectations of establishing an "open-door policy." Set up a workshop to teach employees how to solve ethical dilemmas in the workplace and what HR can do to help solve those issues. Remind employees that HR is not to be feared.

5. Reward good behavior

Bad behavior gets the most attention from HR because we want to try to fix it. What about good behavior? Another way to influence and motivate employees in the workplace is to acknowledge and reward good behavior. While recognizing and rewarding good behavior might sound like a parenting technique, companies will see a positive outcome. A few ways to reward ethical behavior include regular positive feedback, extending the employee's lunch hour, or giving them the rest of the day off on a Friday afternoon. Even a simple, "Hey John, that was a great email you wrote to the VP of Product," creates a positive impact.

As leaders and HR professionals, notice and acknowledge good behavior in employees so that the right employees are moving up the ladder and getting the promotions they deserve. When these employees get into leadership positions, they can continue to create an ethical workplace culture.

6. Partner with ethical vendors

Motivation and influence not only comes from within the company; it can come from working with external vendors. Ethical investing refers to the practice of using an individual or company's values and beliefs as the primary decision to select a company, vendor, or individual to invest in or work with. Working and partnering with vendors that have the same ethics and values in the workplace as your organization is just as important as aligning your executives on core values.

Let's say the CMO of a B2B company decides the marketing team should partner with a 3rd party vendor that brings more attendees to company-hosted events. The marketing and sales team meets with the vendor who has a great track record of high performing events. Before signing a long-term contract, they decide to test the waters and work together on a small roundtable dinner. After a couple of meetings, the marketing team grapples with a number of broken promises the vendor made to collaborate on this project. Instead, they're demanding the marketing team complete the work the vendor was hired to do, and aren't communicating changes in the project scope. The CMO immediately cuts ties with the vendor. While this vendor might've brought great results due to their track record, the behavior toward the marketing team did not align with the company's values and workplace ethics of teamwork, fairness, and humility.

Creating and sustaining types of an ethical workplace culture does not happen overnight; it takes time, effort, and patience. Using core values as the base of building your ideal workplace culture will propel good behavior and prevent any ethical violations that hurt your company. To learn more about creating an ethical workplace, check out our latest video "Creating an Ethical Business Culture."

Ethical Standards

Definition: Ethical standards are a set of principles established by the founders of the organization to communicate its underlying moral values. This code provides a framework that can be used as a reference for decision making processes.

Ethical Standards Mean

These standards are an important part of an organization's culture. They establish the parameters of behavior that owners and top executives expect from employees and also from suppliers, at least to the extent of their relationship with the organization. A corporate governance system will put a lot of effort into communicating and enforcing these principles. This is mostly done through behavior modeling, which means that top executives should set the example of how lower-level employees should act.

A few examples of these standards would be responsibility, honesty, transparency or fairness and even though they might be interpreted differently by each person, companies usually describe the founder's perspective of each value to avoid confusions.

These principles should serve also as guidelines for decision-making processes to help employees align their personal criteria with the company's perspectives as different ethical issues arise within normal business activities. This moral "compass" is crucial to maintain unethical behaviors down to a minimum, mostly in managerial positions.

CHAPTER FOURTEEN

Globalization and Business Ethics

Business ethics is a well-institutionalized academic field, which deals with the moral dimension of business activity. In the context of international business, it means the treating of moral questions of international cultures and countries. International business should be sensitive to the environment and not just selfish for its own profits. Ethically, safety comes first and the profit comes last. The various issues that ethics target are diverse environmental concerns, animal welfare issues, labor practices, fair trade, health concerns, genetic modification, patenting of genes, cloning etc. International business is both more exposed to a variety of ethical conditions as well as in a position to exploit business ethics due to the sheer size an international company has. The end result of an ethical judgment entails its authenticity from being morally correct. But moral correction itself is a relative concept and is based upon the cultural perceptions as well as traditions. The international market and business arena can be ethically segmented into the die hard, the dont cares, and the various groups in between. Companies all around the world are coming under scrutiny from governments, shareholders, customers, trade unions, human-rights groups, and others to prove that their activities are conducted in ethical ways.

Globalization refers to the shift towards a more integrated and interdependent world economy. Globalization has brought a lot of people into contact with the world by declining the barriers of the free flow of goods and services, since the World War II and the dramatic technological change and development in recent years mainly in the past three decades. This development has made the people around the world to be connected to each other. Information and money flow quicker than ever. Products produced in one town are available to the rest of the world. It becomes much easier for anyone to travel, communicate and do business internationally. Free flow of goods and service s has produced many opportunities for business. This whole phenomenon has been called globalization.

Caux Round Table

The Caux Round Table is an international organization of senior business executives aiming to promote ethical business practice. It was founded in 1986 by Frits Philips, president of Philips, and Olivier Giscard d'Estaing, along with Ryuzaburo Kaku, president of Canon.

Frits Philips had been alarmed to hear from reliable sources that the Japanese were dumping their products on the Western market and he feared a growing trade war. He saw the need for trustbuilding between international executives and for Corporate Social Responsibility practices. The CRT's Principles for Business were published in 1994, incorporating western concepts (human dignity...)

and Japanese ones (kyosei, interpreted as "living and working together for the common good"). An international code of good practices written by such senior industrialists from such varied backgrounds remains exceptional today. It was presented to the UN Social Summit in Copenhagen in 1994. It has since become a standard work, translated into 12 languages, and has been used as basis for their internal ethical assessments by international companies such as Nissan.

The CRT's principal activities are an annual meeting and the publication of best-practice guides for various types of organization. Every three years, the annual meeting is held at Caux, Switzerland, where the original initiative took place in 1986. Its chief executive is Stephen B. Young; it has set up chapters in many regions of the world.

Stephen. B. Young is the Global Executive Director of the Caux Round Table, an international network of experienced business leaders who advocate a principled approach to global capitalism. Young has published Moral Capitalism, a well-received book written as a guide to use of the Caux Round Table ethical and socially responsible Principles for Business. In 2008 Prof. Sandra Waddock of the Carroll School of Management of Boston College listed Young among the 23 persons who created the corporate social responsibility movement in her book The Difference Makers.

For the Caux Round Table, Young has partnered with scholars at the International Islamic University of Malaysia to formulate interpretations of Qur'anic guidance for good governance that emphasize the convergence between Qur'an teachings and the global standards advocated by the Caux Round Table.

CRT general principles towards business

Principles

1. **PRINCIPLES FOR RESPONSIBLE BUSINESS**

Seven core principles underlie the Caux Round Table for Moral Capitalism approach to responsible business practices. They are rooted in the recognition that neither the law nor market forces are sufficient to ensure positive and productive – in every sense of the term – conduct.

Principle 1: Respect stakeholders beyond shareholders. A responsible business has responsibilities beyond its investors and managers.

Principle 2: Contribute to economic and social development.

Principle 3: Build trust by going beyond the letter of the law.

Principle 4: Respect rules and conventions.

Principle 5: Support responsible globalization.

Principle 6: Respect the environment.

Principle 7: Avoid illicit activities.

STAKEHOLDER MANAGEMENT GUIDELINES

These guidelines supplement the Principles for Business. They provide specific standards for engaging with key shareholder constituencies. These constituencies are a key to business success and sustainability. In turn, they are the principle beneficiaries of ethical business practices.

Key Stakeholders

Customers: A responsible business treats its customers with respect and dignity.

Employees: This key body of stakeholders owes its well-being to the way employers treat them. Living wages, respect for health and safety and fair wages are all key to a company's long-term success.

Shareholders: A responsible business acts with care and loyalty toward its shareholders.

Suppliers: A responsible business must treat its suppliers with respect and truthfulness. This includes fairness and directness in pricing, licensing and payment.

Competitors: Fair competition is a key to increasing the wealth and stability of an economy. Businesses must promote socially and environmentally responsible behavior with all parties, while avoiding anti-competitive arrangements, respecting tangible and property rights and refusing to acquire commercial information through unethical means.

Communities: Businesses affect public policy and human rights in which they operate. They must do what they can to promote human rights, work with initiatives designed to promote community improvement and sustainable development and support social diversity.

2. PRINCIPLES FOR GOVERNMENT

Bad government is a shortcut to poverty, poor distribution of wealth and chronic civic unrest. We believe better government will attract increased private investment and create more wealth for more people.

Principle 1: Public Power is held in trust for the community. The state is the servant and is subordinate to society.Governments that abuse their power lose their authority and may be removed from office.

Principle 2: Discourse should guide the application of public power. However allocated, public power must abide by the communities of rules, written and/or understood, that guide civil discussion and open decision-making.

Principle 3: Public power constitutes a civic order for the safety and common good of society.

Principle 4: The state shall protect and restore all principles and institutions that sustain the moral integrity and civic identity of citizens. Corruption may not be condoned.

Principle 5: Security of persons, individual liberty and ownership of property are the foundation of individual justice.

Principle 6: Justice shall be provided impartially.

Principle 7: General welfare contemplates improving the well-being of individual citizens. Transparency of government ensures accountability. The more open, the more honest. The more honest, the more legitimate the governing process is viewed by citizens.

Principle 8: Global cooperation advances national welfare. Competition is a vital ingredient – but only one – among countries, as it is among companies.

3. PRINCIPLES FOR GOOD CITIZENSHIP

Human beings can only thrive in community. But that community must be healthy, balanced, fair and equitable with clear rules acknowledged and observed by all members, no matter what their social status. We need the values and courage to live for ourselves and for others in the right balance. True justice is the expression of honest citizenship living in community.

This difficult balancing act is entirely up to our own willingness to learn and live by those principles, even when we personally are not the immediate victor. If we make room for a victory by anyone, then we make room for a victory by all.

Principle 1: I will learn.

Principle 2: I will reflect and deliberate on what I've learned.

Principle 3: I will tell the truth about what I know.

Principle 4: I will not try to hide my ideas and feelings.

Principle 5: I will use my powers wisely.

Principle 6: I will try hard to make the most of my life.

Principle 7: I will not be afraid.

Principle 8: I will care about others.

Principle 9: I will find happiness not in money but in doing what is right.

Principle 10: I will be thankful for all the good I have experienced and brave in times of difficulty and frustration.

4. PRINCIPLES FOR OWNERSHIP OF WEALTH

These days, wealth mostly comes from returns on capital. For capital to behave in an enlightened and sustainable fashion requires that the ownership of wealth must consciously entail a commitment to stewardship.

Principle 1: Wealth should be used to enhance other forms of capital – financial, physical, human, reputational and social.

Principle 2: The desire for self-satisfaction and pride of accomplishment must be balanced against a society's needs to accumulate capital of all kinds.

Principle 3: Wealth must support the creation of social capital.

Principle 4: Wealth should be invested in institutions that enhance social capital, whether that is education or training or other approaches to advance the individual capacity to contribute to the whole.

Principle 5: Private wealth must supplement public expenditures for creating a social safety net.

Principle 6: No one is entitled to use or enjoy wealth procured by fraud, corruption, theft or through other abuses of power.

5. PRINCIPLES FOR NON-GOVERNMENTAL ORGANIZATIONS

Business and government play a leading role in promoting a better world. In recent decades, many Non-Governmental Organizations (NGO) have joined this effort. Some operate on national or transnational terms. Others are only known in their own community. All play a role in ensuring that the rules of moral capitalism and government are enforced.

Principle 1: Integrity. An NGO has to act in accordance with its own code of aspirations.

Principle 2: Public Benefit. An NGO's actions must reflect the values of the people who support the organization, as well as the social, political, economic and environment goals those people support.

Principle 3: Transparency. NGOs should be completely transparent about their mission, objectives, values, principles, governance, actions and means of pursuing its objectives.

Principle 4: Participatory governance. An NGO communicates with the public and stakeholders about its care of transparency, accountability and loyalty in decision-making and fund management.

Principle 5: Independence. An NGO will disclose all ties – financial, political or otherwise – that may affect its impact, intentions and activities.

Principle 6: Respect for the law. This holds both for national and international law.

Principle 7: Care. When engaged in advocacy, planning its actions and executing its policies, an NGO will present truthful information and act with enlightened care for those its policies might affect.

Principle 8: Accountability. An NGO will produce, on a regular basis, a public, web-based report on all the activities it has taken to realize its mission and objectives

CHAPTER FIFTEEN

Stakeholder, Employee, Owner

A stakeholder is a party that has an interest in a company and can either affect or be affected by the business. The primary stakeholders in a typical corporation are its investors, employees, customers, and suppliers.

However, with the increasing attention on corporate social responsibility, the concept has been extended to include communities, governments, and trade associations.

KEY TAKEAWAYS:

- A stakeholder has a vested interest in a company and can either affect or be affected by a business' operations and performance.
- Typical stakeholders are investors, employees, customers, suppliers, communities, governments, or trade associations.
- An entity's stakeholders can be both internal or external to the organization.

Understanding Stakeholders

Stakeholders can be internal or external to an organization. Internal stakeholders are people whose interest in a company comes through a direct relationship, such as employment, ownership, or investment.

External stakeholders are those who do not directly work with a company but are affected somehow by the actions and outcomes of the business. Suppliers, creditors, and public groups are all considered external stakeholders.

Example of an Internal Stakeholder

Investors are internal stakeholders who are significantly impacted by the associated concern and its performance. If, for example, a venture capital firm decides to invest $5 million in a technology startup in return for 10% equity and significant influence, the firm becomes an internal stakeholder of the startup.

The return on the venture capitalist firm's investment hinges on the startup's success or failure, meaning that the firm has a vested interest.

Example of an External Stakeholder

External stakeholders, unlike internal stakeholders, do not have a direct relationship with the company. Instead, an external stakeholder is normally a person or organization affected by the operations of the business. When a company goes over the allowable limit of carbon emissions, for example, the town in which the company is located is considered an external stakeholder because it is affected by the increased pollution.

Conversely, external stakeholders may also sometimes have a direct effect on a company without a clear link to it. The government, for example, is an external stakeholder. When the government initiates policy changes on carbon emissions, the decision affects the business operations of any entity with increased levels of carbon.

Problems With Stakeholders

A common problem that arises for companies with numerous stakeholders is that the various stakeholder interests may not align. In fact, the interests may be in direct conflict. For example, the primary goal of a corporation, from the perspective of its shareholders, is to maximize profits and enhance shareholder value. Since labor costs are unavoidable for most companies, a company may seek to keep these costs under tight control. This is likely to upset another group of stakeholders, its employees. The most efficient companies successfully manage the interests and expectations of all their stakeholders.

Stakeholders vs. Shareholders

Stakeholders are bound to a company by some type of vested interest, usually for the long term and for reasons of need. Meanwhile, a shareholder has a financial interest, but a shareholder can sell a stock and buy different stock or keep the proceeds in cash; they do not have a long-term need for the company and can get out at any time.

For example, if a company is performing poorly financially, the vendors in that company's supply chain might suffer if the company limits production and no longer uses its services. Similarly, employees of the company might lose their jobs. However, shareholders of the company can sell their stock and limit their losses.

Examples of Stakeholders

Examples of important stakeholders for a business include its shareholders, customers, suppliers, and employees. Some of these stakeholders, such as the shareholders and the employees, are internal to the business. Others, such as the business's customers and suppliers, are external to the business but are nevertheless affected by the business's actions. These days, it has become more common to talk about a broader range of external stakeholders, such as the government of the countries in which the business operates, or even the public at large.

Are Stakeholders Important?

Stakeholders are important for a number of reasons. For internal stakeholders, they are important because the business's operations rely on their ability to work together toward the business's goals. External stakeholders on the other hand can affect the business indirectly.

For instance, customers can change their buying habits, suppliers can change their manufacturing and distribution practices, and governments can modify laws and regulations. Ultimately, managing relationships with internal and external stakeholders is key to a business's long-term success.

Are Stakeholders and Shareholders the Same?

Although shareholders are an important type of stakeholder, they are not the only stakeholders. Examples of other stakeholders include employees, customers, suppliers, governments, and the public at large. In recent years, there has been a trend toward thinking more broadly about who constitutes the stakeholders of a business.

Employee

An employee is someone who gets paid to work for a person or company.

Workers don't need to work full time to be considered employees—they simply need to be paid to work by an employer (the person or business that pays them). The term employee is sometimes used to distinguish contract workers from full employees (who often earn additional benefits), but in this example, both types of workers are considered employees in the general sense.

Example: My company has more than 500 employees.

Investors

Many people use the words "trading" and "investing" interchangeably when, in reality, they are two very different activities. While both traders and investors participate in the same marketplace, they perform two very different tasks using very different strategies. Both of these roles are necessary, however, for the market to function smoothly. This article will take a look at both parties and the strategies they use to make a profit in the marketplace.

KEY TAKEAWAYS

- Investors and traders have different objectives, different strategies and different methods of approaching financial markets.
- Investors tend to be focused on the long-term, seeking to put money in securities that are both profitable and appear to represent a good value.
- The largest investors are investment banks, mutual funds, institutional investors, and retail investors.
- Traders are also market participants, but they often have a shorter time horizon and are looking for price fluctuations in a stock relative to the market, rather than buying into a security for the long-term.
- Traders take their cues from price patterns, supply and demand, market emotion, and client services.
- Major traders include investment banks, market makers, arbitrage funds, and proprietary traders and firms.

What Is an Investor?

An investor is the market participant the general public most often associates with the stock market. Investors are those who purchase shares of a company for the long term with the belief that the company has strong future prospects. Investors typically concern themselves with two things:

- Value: Investors must consider whether a company's shares represent a good value. For example, if two similar companies are trading at different earnings multiples, the lower one might be the better value because it suggests that the investor will need to pay less for $1 of earnings when investing in Company A relative to what would be needed to gain exposure to $1 of earnings in Company B.
- Success: Investors must measure the company's future success by looking at its financial strength and evaluating its future cash flows.

Both of these factors can be determined through the analysis of the company's financial statements along with a look at industry trends that may define future growth prospects. At a basic level, investors can measure the current value of a company relative to its future growth possibilities by looking at metrics such as the PEG ratio: that is, the company's P/E (value) to growth (success) ratio.

Major Investors

There are many different investors that are active in the marketplace. In fact, the vast majority of the money that is at work in the markets belongs to investors (not to be confused with the number of dollars traded per day, which is a record held by the traders). Major investors include:

Investment Banks: Investment banks are organizations that assist companies in going public and raising money. This often involves holding at least a portion of the securities over the long term.

Mutual Funds: Many individuals keep their money in mutual funds, which make long-term investments in companies that meet specific criteria. Mutual funds are required by law to act as investors, not traders.

Institutional Investors: These are large organizations or persons that hold large stakes in companies. Institutional investors often include company insiders, competitors hedging themselves and special opportunity investors.

Retail Investors: Retail investors are individuals that invest in the stock market for their personal accounts. At first, the influence of retail traders may seem small, but as time passes more people are taking control of their portfolios and, as a result, the influence of this group is increasing.

All of these parties are looking to hold positions for the long term in an effort to stick with the company while continuing to be successful. Warren Buffett's success is a testament to the viability of this strategy.

Supplier

A supplier is an entity that supplies goods and services to another organization. This entity is part of the supply chain of a business, which may provide the bulk of the value contained within its products. Some suppliers may even engage in drop shipping, where they ship goods directly to the customers of the buyer.

A supplier is usually a manufacturer or a distributor. A distributor buys goods from multiple manufacturers and sells them to its customers.

Example of a Supplier

A shoe manufacturer buys components for its shoes from a group of suppliers. One supplier provides it with rubber heels, while another supplier provides it with tanned leather. A third supplier provides it with the buckles to be used on selected shoe models, while a fourth supplier provides the thread used to stitch shoes together.

Community

The definition of community is all the people living in an area or a group or groups of people who share common interests. ... A group of people living together or in the same locality or who share interests or a sense of identity.

CHAPTER SIXTEEN

Environmental Ethics

Environmental ethics is a branch of ethics that studies the relation of human beings and the environment and how ethics play a role in this. Environmental ethics believe that humans are a part of society as well as other living creatures, which includes plants and animals. These items are a very important part of the world and are considered to be a functional part of human life.

Therefore, it is essential that every human being respected and honor this and use morals and ethics when dealing with these creatures.

According to Wikipedia,

"In environmental philosophy, environmental ethics is an established field of practical philosophy "which reconstructs the essential types of argumentation that can be made for protecting natural entities and the sustainable use of natural resources." The main competing paradigms are anthropocentrism, physiocentrism (called ecocentrism as well), and theocentrism. Environmmental ethics exerts influence on a large range of disciplines including environmental law, environmental sociology, ecotheology, ecological economics, ecology and environmental geography."

Global warming, global climate change, deforestation, pollution, resource degradation, the threat of extinction are few of the issues from which our planet is suffering. Environmental ethics are a key feature of environmental studies that establishes the relationship between humans and the earth. With environmental ethics, you can ensure that you are doing your part to keep the environment safe and protected.

Every time that a tree is cut down to make a home or other resources are used, we are using natural resources that are becoming more and more sparse to find. It is essential that you do your part to keep the environment protected and free from danger. It is not as difficult to do as you may think so long as you're willing to make a few simple and easy changes.

With the rapid increase in the world's population, the consumption of natural resources has increased several times. This has degraded our planet's ability to provide the services we humans need. The consumption of resources is going at a faster rate than they can naturally replenish.

Environmental ethics builds on scientific understanding by bringing human values, moral principles, and improved decision making into conversation with science. It was Earth Day in 1970 that helped to develop environmental ethics in the US, and soon thereafter, the same ethics were developed in other countries, including Canada and North America. This is important because the ethics of the environment are of major concern these days.

Environmental Ethics and Its Principles

There are several approaches or principles to determine how we are to value our environment. It is such a huge field, and it is so vast that it is difficult for one principle to cover all the ground. Many theories have emerged over the years, and each one has stressed on various principles of environmental ethics. The list below states all the principles that have been predominantly found in those theories.

1. Anthropocentrism

It suggests that human beings are the most important beings. All other living beings are but accessories that would assist in their survival. Now, there are two further divisions of anthropocentrism. They are weak anthropocentrism and strong anthropocentrism.

While weak anthropocentrism believes that human beings are the centre because it is only through their perspective that environmental situations can be interpreted.

Strong anthropocentrism, however, believes that human beings are at the centre because they rightfully deserve to be there. Peter Vardy made this distinction.

2. Non-Anthropocentrism

As opposed to anthropocentrism, non-anthropocentrism, this principle gives value to every object, every animal in nature. It is a principle that believes in everything that sustains itself in nature.

3. Psychocentrism

Psychocentrism is the principle that believes that human beings hold more value in the environment since their mental capacities are better developed and far more complex than any other element in the environment.

4. Biocentrism

It is a term that holds not only an ecological but also a political value. It is a philosophy that imparts importance to all living beings. In terms of environmental ethics, biocentrism is the principle that ensures the proper balance of ecology on the planet.

5. Holism

The term holism had been coined by Jan Smuts in his book called Holism and Evolution (1926). Holism considers environment systems as a whole rather than being individual parts of something. It considers these environment systems to be valuable.

6. Resourcism

The principle of resourcism says that nature is considered to be valuable only because it has resources to provide with. Thus, nature ought to be exploited.

7. Speciesism

The principle of speciesism justifies the superiority of the human race. Thus, it also justifies the exploitation and maltreatment of animals by humankind.

8. Moral Considerability

This, too, is an important principle of environmental ethics. Intrinsic value is added to every being, which makes us consider being moral. Moral considerability towards a being means that we agree that all our interactions whatsoever with the being is bound by moral laws.

9. Instrumental Value

The instrumental value is the value imparted to a being as long as it can serve us with resources.

10. Intrinsic Value

Intrinsic value is the value attached to a being just for itself and not only for its resourcefulness.

11. Aesthetic Value

Aesthetic value is imparted to a being by virtue of its looks or its beauty.

12. Animal Liberation or Animal Rights

As is evident from its name, animal liberation or rights try to secure animal life and ensure their welfare by enforcing certain laws.

13. Animal Welfare

It ensures that the animals are treated well and humanely.

Types of Environmental Ethics

With the emergence of several theories, several environmental ethics have emerged. While some protect human beings, others protect plants, animals and other elements of nature. The types include:

- Social ecology, which is the study of human beings and their relation to their environment.
- Deep ecology promotes that all beings have an intrinsic value.
- Ecofeminism is a branch of feminism that helps us look at earth as a woman so that we can respect it in a better way.

CHAPTER SEVENTEEN

Marketing Ethics

Marketing Ethics or Ethical Marketing is one of the most effective long-term branding, word-of-mouth, and trust-building strategies for optimizing presence, leads, sales, and conversions of a product or service.

Marketing ethics revolves around those principles of ethical marketing and standards that guide acceptable marketing conduct.

Ethical marketing is an integral part of the marketing definition that the American Marketing Association suggests, which is-

Marketing is the activity, set of institutions, and processes for creating, communicating, delivering, and exchanging offerings that have value for customers, clients, partners, and society at large.

Here, offering values to customers, partners, clients, and society is the core essence of an ethical marketing campaign.

Marketing Ethics ?

Ethics in marketing involves the marketing practices of promoting fairness, social responsibility, empathy, and honesty by following ethical standards.

From marketing tactics to marketing decisions and advertising of products and services, all the ethical marketing practices focus not only on how products would benefit users but also on how they fulfill social responsibility and handle different ethical issues.

These affect consumers' benefits and the benefits they take away from related environmental and social causes. It is a philosophy on top of strategy and is instrumental to both the company and its consumers.

Through ethical marketing, organizations deliberately apply different sets of moral rights and fairness standards when marketing their products and services, practices, and behavior in the overall structure. These organizations can then develop a competitive advantage over time, thereby satisfying the organization's needs and customers.

Marketing Ethics Important

As per stats, 90+% of millennial consumers prefer buying products from ethical companies. Also, more than 80% of those users think that ethical brands outperform other market players that do follow ethical marketing.

Ethical marketing is essential to the overall growth and development of an organization over time.

The applied set of guidelines and rules paves the way for a morally good, organized roadmap for everyone to follow. These sometimes overlap with media ethics since they are closely related in terms of definition and functioning.

The following are the reasons why ethical marketing is an integral part of the life of an organization:

1. Long-term gains

The foundation of a company or organization is not just based on its ability to survive the present, but to plan a bright future.

With the adoption of proper marketing ethics, brands can employ prospects like high credibility, loyalty to customers, significant market share, increased brand value, better sales, and better revenue.

These ethical practices will put their right on their way towards the accomplishment of both short-term and long-term goals with perfection.

2. Customer Loyalty

This is one of the most important factors when it comes to ethical marketing.

With the proper adoption of ethics in terms of business and operation, the company can win the loyalty, trust, and confidence of its consumers that can go a long way into the future.

The natural human tendency to go after the genuine brand will surely give them promising gains, both in the present and in the future.

3. Increased credibility

When the organization looks forward to keeping its promises surrounding its services and products on a continuous and consistent basis, it slowly and steadily goes towards the path of carving itself into an authentic and genuine brand in the market and customers' minds.

This is not just limited to these two, and a good process can even build good respect in front of investors, peers, competitors, stakeholders, etc.

4. Increased Leadership qualities

When a company follows ethical practices of ethics for an extended period, it gradually stations itself as a leader, one who can benchmark its policies and strategies that surround the company's structure and functioning.

This eventually gives rise to numerous benefits like increased share in the market, higher sales, inspiration for others, respect, mutual benefits, etc.

5. The satisfaction of basic human wants and needs

Once an organization is on course for the proper marketing ethics, it solves the basic needs and wants of its consumers in the form of integrity, trust, and honesty.

When this is displayed for a long time, various other benefits follow.

6. Display of a rich culture

Not only does such a structure give a positive outlook when seen from the outside, but it also paves the way for a good structure and environment within the hierarchy internally.

This gives rise to higher production owing to a confident and highly motivated staff.

7. The attraction of the right talent at the right place

Once the company can create brand value in the market, it becomes a beacon for prominent individuals for the association.

Various people like prospective employees, consultants, vendors, etc. look forward to associating and working with the ethical brands that boost them exponentially. This further helps them in achieving their goals in a short period successfully.

8. Reaching financial goals

To function smoothly for more extended periods, the company has to have good financial partners who can help them grow and make significant strides in the market.

Once the brand follows a proper set of rules and ethical guidelines, it helps them earn the moral ground necessary to attract such people.

9. Enhancement of brand value in the market

Once a proper code concerning ethical marketing is followed by the organization, the public in the form of customers, competitors, stakeholders, etc. look up to such organizations. They follow such brands with religious dedication, giving them sufficient boost to mark the market.

Role of Ethics in Marketing

With time, our economic system has become sufficient at providing wants and needs for the public.

This has shifted the main focus of the market with an inclination towards ethical values while serving the needs of customers. This is primarily due to two reasons:

When there is ethical behavior from the organization's side, there is a more significant positive public attitude to the variety of services and goods they offer. They have to adhere to specific marketing standards to render their efforts valid to the general public.

In addition to this, ethical bodies and organizations tend to pressurize and hold organizations and companies accountable for their actions. There is a lot of questioning and sets of guidelines, which have to be strictly followed.

Ethics in marketing plays a key role in ethical decision making crucial for the optimized presence of a product or service in their target niche.

An ethical marketing strategy is responsible for paying heed upon different factors such as-

- Organization factors such as culture, norms, values, and opportunity
- Individual factors such as moral philosophies and values
- Stakeholder interests and concerns
- The intensity of ethical issues in marketing and organization setup

- Ethical decision making
- Evaluation of ethical outcomes

CHAPTER EIGHTEEN

Ethical Issues in Human Resource Management

Business ethics are the moral doctrines that direct the way to business behave. Business ethics determines the actions of every individual that distinguish the right or wrong. Every business organization must develop the codes of conduct and ethics that should be followed by all the members. Ethics can be taken as the crucial way to self-presentation and public perception of the organization. Ethics in human resource management is related to the employee's issues. Human resource management plays an important role in setting up and implementing ethics in the workplace. Implementation of ethics in the workplace has been one of the challenging tasks for the organization. Various human resources issues can be handled properly by the application of ethics and code of practices by the managers in the workplace. Ethics generally determine what is right and what is wrong. With the help of business ethics, proper allocation and maintenance of employee in the workplace will be possible.

The Ethical Concern in Human Resource Management

Human resource management plays a vital role in the organization while dealing with workplace issues. As human resource management deals with the management of human resources in the workplace, the issues related with the human resource must be focused by the top level management. The major ethical issues that have to be deal by the human resource management are a concern with the privacy issues, cash and compensation plan, employment issues, safety issues, race and disability, performance appraisal and employee's responsibility. Each and every employee is important for the organization to achieve the stated goal so the issues related with the manpower must be identified on time for the better performance. In a workplace, there will be a good and bad work performance with the application of right ethical theory the human issues can be managed. For the effective outcomes, all the employees must be treated ethically. Employment issues are the general issues faced by the organization as an individual belongs to different background, culture, religion, and races. So, hiring an employee creates a dilemma for the HR managers. The presentation of fake documents during the time of hiring may cause a problem in the future so, ethical action is the most essential aspects that should be adopted by both parties. HR manager must provide an equal opportunity and treatment for the individual while hiring.

Another human resource management issue is related to privacy. All the employees in the organization have their own personal life. The information may be related to religion, social beliefs and many more. An employee wants to maintain the privacy within the organization so they want the direct and indirect protection from the company. So, without the permission of employee privacy should not be leaked. Such an unethical act should not be conducted by the organization. Most of the time people are treated badly in the workplace in the name of race, gender, and disability. The ethics-based organization should not focus on discrimination while the employees should be appreciated for their contribution to the organization. Similarly, an employee should be compensated on the basis of their performance. A company must have an effective compensating plan for their employees. The general ethical issues involved while managing the human resource is related to the salaries, executive benefits, and compensation including the annual incentives, flexible working hours, holidays and many more. Compensating the employee for their contribution is one of the ethics that can be adopted by the organization. This action increases the morale of employees and increases performance. Along with the other responsibilities safety of employees is also one of the burning issues of human resource management. Employee's safety in the workplace is the ethical as well as the human right that should be provided by the organization. It is one of the sensitive factors that cannot be avoided by the organization to their employees.

For the effective management of human resource in the workplace, ethics must be considered by the managers. Effective implementation of the ethic helps in controlling the human resources in a right way. Without the ethics in the workplace, there will not be the better performance rather it will decrease the morale of the employee and gradually increase the turnover in the organization. Thus, for the satisfaction of the employee within the organization, the business ethics is essential to adopt by the company. Ethical demand in the workplace is the concern of the human resource management in the present context. Ethics in the workplace provides employee's right and well-being. Since, the success or failure of the business totally depends upon the ethical behavior shown by the managers in the organization. For the success of the organization, management must adopt the consistence ethical behavior to all the employees in the workplace. The ethical behavior of managers in workplace changes the behavior of the employee such as a change in attitude, interest and get motivated to perform the activities.

9 798885 467605

Printed by Libri Plureos GmbH in Hamburg, Germany